THE
CONSCIOUSNESS
OF THE
LITIGATOR

THE

CONSCIOUSNESS

OF THE

LITIGATOR

Duffy Graham

THE UNIVERSITY OF MICHIGAN PRESS
Ann Arbor

2008   2007   2006   2005   4   3   2   1

A CIP catalog record for this book is available from the British Library.

Library of Congress Cataloging-in-Publication Data

Graham, Duffy.
The consciousness of the litigator / Duffy Graham.
p.   cm.
Includes bibliographical references and index.
ISBN 0-472-11500-6 (cloth : alk. paper)
1. Practice of law—Moral and ethical aspects—United States.
2. Actions and defenses—Moral and ethical aspects—United States.
3. Attorney and client—Moral and ethical aspects—United States.
4. Legal ethics—United States.   5. Lawyers—United States.
I. Title.

KF306.G724   2005
174'.3'0973—dc22   2004023738

For
Jan Deutsch
and
Robert Jackall

CONTENTS

ACKNOWLEDGMENTS

The author will always be grateful to the following individuals for various and invaluable contributions to this book: Jan Deutsch, Robert Jackall, Jim Reische, Arthur J. Vidich, and each of the attorneys who participated in the field interviews.

INTRODUCTION

This book examines the moral consciousness of the litigator, the quintessential modern lawyer. The primary skill of the litigator is the fundamental skill of all lawyers, making legal arguments, and the litigator's work extends to every corner of society.

The term *litigator* identifies a type of lawyer. The term is descriptive and shorthand. It suggests certain occupational tendencies, but, at the margins, the work from one litigator to the next varies in particulars and emphases.

The main task of the litigator is to provide legal representation to parties in lawsuits filed in the courts, but the litigator also provides other legal services. He assists clients in resolving or attempting to resolve disputes outside of the format of lawsuits. He represents parties in arbitration, mediation, and other specialized extrajudicial proceedings. He argues cases before appellate courts on appeal from trial—an activity that occurs within the framework of a lawsuit but that is not a routine part of the litigator's work. He appears in administrative and legislative hearings. He works to resolve conflicts informally. He also maneuvers through the obstacle course of government and corporate bureaucracies to obtain information for a client. He occasionally drafts and negotiates agreements—work that typically lies in the province of those generally known as business lawyers—and often provides substantive advice in one or another specialized area of law. He finds himself now and then working in some never-never land far removed from filing a motion to dismiss or taking a deposition. Still, the main job of the litigator is representing clients in lawsuits.

The litigator's work lies almost entirely within civil, as opposed to criminal, law. It occasionally involves criminal issues, but criminal defense work is different and likely calls for a specialist in that area.

The litigator may represent either side in a lawsuit—the plaintiff or the defendant. The litigator represents any party to civil litigation, including individuals, sole proprietorships, partnerships, corporations, nonprofit organizations, quasi-governmental agencies, and government departments and agencies.

The litigator is a generalist with respect to subject matter and types of legal claims. He takes pride in his ability to handle any subject matter that comes through the door in the form of a lawsuit, whether a labor and employment dispute, consumer law matter, antitrust issue, professional malpractice, or intellectual property dispute, to name only a few beyond bread-and-butter contract and tort matters. As a practical matter, not every litigator does work in every subject area, and some end up specializing in a single area. Those lawyers whose work is predominantly or exclusively in specialized kinds of litigation are litigators, but their professional identities likely reflect those specialties—for example, environmental litigator or intellectual property litigator.

The main job encompasses representing parties at trial, and over a career most litigators do "go to trial." In practice, though, few litigators are true trial lawyers. Most could only say fairly that they have done trial work. For multiple and complex reasons, most civil lawsuits never reach trial, and the bulk of the litigator's work lies outside of trial, mostly in the pretrial stages of a lawsuit. Pretrial work does involve "going to court" in the form of appearing before judges to argue motions and to manage the progress of cases.

The litigator is a specialist in civil procedure. A lawsuit proceeds according to rules. The rules that govern how a lawsuit proceeds, including especially the pretrial stages, are the rules of civil procedure. The federal court system and the state court systems all have their own formal set of rules of civil procedure. Every court has its own practice rules, too, governing every question from deadlines to the width of margins for papers filed with the court to the color of the ink required for an attorney's signature.

All cases proceed from the filing of the complaint toward final judgment. Most cases never reach final judgment—along the way the judge may dismiss them, for example, or the parties may agree to settle the case. Once a party files a complaint, however, the case must reach some sort of disposition: once a party engages the court, the administrative imperatives of the court require that the case be resolved.

The filing of a complaint does not mean that, under the law, a wrong has been committed or harm has been done. It means that a claim of wrongdoing and harm is being made. After the complaint is filed, the litigator devotes his efforts to persuading the court to decide the case in his client's favor. Toward that end, the litigator spends most of his time developing facts and legal arguments.

In litigation, facts are determinations that have legal consequences. At the beginning of every case, no facts are assumed or given. The litigator seeks to establish facts that support the client's legal arguments. He also seeks to prevent the establishment of facts that would support the other party's legal arguments. Most of the fact development occurs through what is known as the discovery process. In discovery, the parties to the lawsuit endeavor to obtain from each other or from third parties information that may be relevant to the lawsuit. Discovery rules aim to leave the parties to themselves to obtain information from each other, but commonly the parties must ask the court to intervene and give orders regarding what must and must not be done. Discovery is the trench warfare of litigation. The rules of civil procedure provide formal discovery methods, such as oral depositions of witnesses, requests for documents, and written interrogatories or questions, but every question, every request—including every word of every question or request—is subject to resistance. The resistance is sometimes groundless, sometimes legitimate.

The litigator does not take information obtained through discovery and from other sources at face value. The litigator seeks to give the information meaning, possibly even by challenging what it appears to mean. In litigation, a fact is not a fact until the court says it is—a statement, a document, an event does not have legal consequences until the court finds that it does. If a witness states that *x happened,* and if whether *x happened* is a significant issue, the litigator for one side may try to support the statement with other information and contend that the statement establishes certain facts—for example, that indeed *x happened* or that *y did not happen.* The litigator for the other side may try to discredit or to nullify the statement that *x happened* by eliciting contradictory or qualifying statements from the same witness or by finding other witnesses who state *not x* or documents that tend to disprove *x happened.* The litigator subjects statements and words in a written document—such as those in a contract, a memo, an invoice—as well as the document itself to the same degree of scrutiny.

In litigation, the law is the rule that determines the outcome of a disputed issue. In each case and with respect to each issue in the case, the law is not assumed, or given, either. Every case creates new law, if only by reapplying an agreed-upon rule to the new facts that every case presents. The distinction between applying an established rule to new facts and creating a new rule is often fuzzy. The litigator seeks to persuade the court regarding what law applies and why application of the law favors his client. Developing legal arguments entails marshaling authorities, such as statutes, regulations, decisions in previous cases, and treatises and other pro-fessional commentaries, and considering their applica-tion to the facts of the case. Making a legal argument to the court entails presenting those authorities and demonstrating why those authorities, in light of the facts, require a certain outcome. The litigator seeks to construct legal arguments that both support the client's position and destroy the legal arguments advanced by the other parties. The litigator does not, of course, take a legal authority at face value. Instead, he seeks to give it meaning. He makes an argument as to what the author-ity means and why it supports his client's position, undermines the opposing party's position, or does not apply to the situation. Sometimes he argues that the existing authority is wrong and needs to be changed.

In each case, facts and legal arguments are mutually dependent: development of one affects development of the other. The litigator seeks to develop facts that sup-port application of a certain rule and to develop arguments that favor certain facts. Sometimes the facts turn out to be other than what the litigator thought they were or what the client said they were, so the litigator must adjust the legal argument accordingly or develop a different one. Sometimes the law turns out to be other than what the litigator thought it was, and so the litigator seeks to develop different facts or impart to the facts a different meaning. Usually a measure of both processes is under way at all times.

In short, the litigator spends his time both challenging and constructing apparent meaning by assiduously examining context. He takes nothing for granted, not even what seems most immutable in support of his own client's position.

Representing a party to a civil lawsuit requires not only searching for and questioning witnesses and obtaining and analyzing written documents, but also learning the ins and outs of individual lives, organizations, industries, economies, and particular social worlds. It also requires standing up for the rights and interests of the client against the opposing party and before a judge. Representing a party to a civil lawsuit benefits from eloquence and precision in verbal and written communication, creative thinking, fortitude, political savvy, and the exercise of good judgment. It may also benefit from a good deal of nerve.

By way of this occupation, the litigator has access to an array of major economic and government institutions, the individuals who animate them, and especially the information, expertise, and power, both principled and arbitrary, that these institutions and individuals have at their disposal. The work takes the litigator through the courts, judges' chambers, and other lawyers' offices; government agencies and the offices of policymakers and policy enforcers; the executive offices and physical plants of corporations; and the administrative apparatuses that support these institutions. The investigative, confrontational, and cooperative imperatives of the work lead the litigator to plumb the logic of institutions and the psyches of individuals. The litigator routinely witnesses and mediates the complex, ordinary and extraordinary, social, political, economic, and legal transactions that occur variously among private individuals, private and public organizations, and local, state, and federal government—day in, day out across the country.

The job carries heavy responsibility. The filing of a civil lawsuit is commonplace but dreadful.[1] Even in a relatively minor suit, careers, livelihoods, reputations, self-images, customs and practices and policies, the survival of organizations, time, resources, and money—lots of money—can be at stake. A lawsuit is expensive and inefficient. It also invokes the awesome power of the courts.

The litigator, like other lawyers, often hears himself described as a Hired Gun. The tone with which the term is invoked is usually contemptuous—except that one who stands to benefit from the Hired Gun's services sounds a more temperate, possibly gleeful note. The tone is also always distanced. The distance maintained results less from distrust of the Hired Gun's outsider origins or resentment over his expertise or his pay than from concern about his morality. The Hired Gun appears to be immoral to the extent that he appears to allow payment to determine what conduct is right—and therefore what conduct he will undertake. He appears to believe that what is right is what is in his employer's interests. The Hired Gun appears to be amoral to the extent that he appears to act without reference to right and wrong, or without determining for himself what is right under the circumstances and acting accordingly. The classic image of the lawyer as Hired Gun is the criminal defense lawyer whose interest seems to be to help the client either get away with a crime of which the client is guilty or "get off" without regard to the issue of innocence or guilt—that is, "on a technicality." The litigator has a less public yet similar image. The litigator appears motivated to promote the client's interests, especially through use of technical and obscure legal rules, without concern for issues of responsibility. The litigator appears to have no moral center and to adopt or to accept passively the moral view of the client. Inasmuch as the litigator appears to think and act as a function of the client's interests, he appears to see right and wrong as a function of the client's interests.

The structure of the occupation provides inducements for the litigator to see right and wrong strictly through the lens of the client's interests. The adversary system, lawyers' professional ethical rules, the legal profession's self-promotion, basic societal demands, and the agreement between the litigator and the client for providing representation all cast the litigator in the role of the client's representative before the court in a lawsuit: Under the adversary system, the job of the litigator is to represent the client's position regarding facts, what legal rules should apply, and what the outcome of the dispute should be, not to represent the interests of other parties to the dispute or the interests of outsiders, not to decide what legal rules apply, not to decide the outcome of the case, and not to determine what the law should be. The main thrust of lawyers' rules of professional conduct is loyalty to and zealous advocacy on behalf of the client, within broad limits.[2] The profession endlessly portrays itself as the devoted advocate at law for the client, and, reciprocally, society demands that the lawyer guide and protect the client through and against the mysterious mechanisms of the law. Given the dependence of the client, the competing interests of other parties to the lawsuit, the power of the courts, the ever-changing nature of the law, and the watchful and opportunistic eye of outside parties and the general public, representing the client's interests in a lawsuit is a rough-and-tumble, exhausting task. The thorough empathy for the client required by the litigator's role tempts the litigator to understand right and wrong exclusively in terms of the client's perceived interests. Indeed, the adversary system, the ethical rules, and other structural demands, as well as the ever-present client, provide ready-made moral justifications for the litigator's conduct and decision making. The litigator can always point to these obligations and claim that what is right is what's right for the client.

In some instances, the structural pressures on the litigator come very near to determining the litigator's sense of right and wrong, to making right be whatever is in the client's interest.

> There may be situations where I'm working on a case, and if I were to put aside ethical rules and all the rules that we deal with, all the technical rules and all the things we deal with, you kind of look at the case or you look at some set of facts and you think, gee, here's what a really fair—this might be a fair outcome here. But because the other side hasn't done their homework properly, or because

the way the law actually works, it actually works in your favor, even if it's not the exact fair outcome—you don't sell your client short on that. I don't.

Suppose a client is sued under a certain statute, and I think the statute is probably a good statute, something we ought to have. Well, if the client thinks it's a bad statute, and there are arguments for us to say this is a bad statute and it's either unconstitutional or it shouldn't apply here or we can come up with whatever arguments we can to either wipe out the statute or diminish it or restrict it, well, then, we do that, because our ultimate obligation as lawyers is to provide our client with the best legal service we can. And if there's room in the law to try to let us reshape the law or move the law, even if it's not entirely consistent with what we think the outcome ought to be, then I do that. . . .

That's what [clients are] really paying for, for really big cases, for the 5 percent of really creative thinking to try to push things in one direction or the other. And sometimes you end up doing that, you may end up shaping the law in something that is very good for your client, but maybe in the bigger picture, for society, is maybe not the right way to push the law. But if the legislature wants to deal with that, it will. That's kind of how I see it.*

In practice, however, the occupational role and the client's interests inform but do not determine the litigator's moral consciousness. The litigator's sense of right

* *Throughout the book, all quotations of litigators are taken from interviews conducted by the author for this study. See the Author's Note for a description of the data.*

and wrong is not so wooden as to be entirely constructed from rules and other structural forces, not so malleable as to be simply a function of the client's interests. Rather, the experience of the work defines the shape and content of the litigator's moral consciousness.

An understanding of the moral consciousness of the litigator requires a grasp of the sociopolitical and institutional contexts of his work. Part 1 of this book attempts to provide handles on these contexts. Chapter 1 explores the role of the lawyer in American society. The litigator is first and foremost a lawyer, and the role lawyers always have played in American society is indispensable. The political design of American society requires lawyers to make it work. Chapter 2 explores the judicial process. The whole of the litigator's main task occurs within the province of the courts. The litigator seeks ultimately to convince the courts that his client's position is correct under the law. The role of lawyers and the judicial process inform the litigator's daily experience, which shapes his consciousness. Part 2 explores that consciousness. It plumbs the litigator's understanding of himself, his work, and especially his sense of right and wrong.

Lawyers' performance of their role and judicial decision making promote both order and disorder in American society. Lawyers and the judicial process help to hold society together: They bind disparate interests to each other and to society through the mechanism of law. They legitimate interests, alleviate conflict, and define social relationships and responsibilities. In so doing, however, lawyers and the judicial process also help to disrupt society: Every legitimation of an interest and every resolution of conflict creates new circumstances to which elements in society must adjust. Every definition of a

relationship or responsibility changes existing relationships and obligations. In short, every effort through law
to achieve repose results in disquiet.

The litigator instinctively understands this para-
dox—it is the social wellspring of his work. Litigation
practice shapes a consciousness that takes into account
the complexity and ever-shifting nature of social life, is
skeptical of surface appearances and public claims, and
makes judgment of right and wrong in any given
instance a matter of precision.

PART ONE

The Context of the Litigator's Work

CHAPTER ONE

The Lawyer in American Society

The first person to see lawyers as a unique occupational group in American society was Alexis de Tocqueville. His observations on the American legal profession appeared in volume 1 of *Democracy in America,* published in 1835.

Tocqueville undertook his study of American political and social institutions out of abiding concern for the future of France and, more immediately, alarm over the July Revolution in 1830 and the crowning of Louis Philippe, the "Citizen King."[1] From the moment in 1788 when Louis XVI summoned the Estates-General, unleashing the forces that destroyed the ancien régime, through the Terror and the short-lived First Republic, the Napoleonic Wars, the restoration of the Bourbons and the reactionary policies of Charles X, to the barricades of the July Revolution, France experienced uncertainty and violent upheaval. When Tocqueville set about to write *Democracy in America,* the promise of the Revolution of 1789 remained unfulfilled, and France stood, mired and confused, between the old regime and the modern world.

The scheme of life during the centuries of the old regime was orderly. It featured a hereditary monarchy and three classes or estates—the commoners, the clergy, and the nobility. The commoners consisted of the peasants, small merchants, and the bourgeoisie. The 1789 Revolution swept aside the premises and eradicated the structural divisions of the old order. It dismantled the hereditary aristocracy and introduced an elected legislature and equality before the law.

Tocqueville's family had belonged to the noble class under the old regime. During the Terror of 1793, several members of his mother's family, including his maternal great-grandfather, Malesherbes, who had stepped forward to defend Louis XVI at the latter's trial, were executed. Tocqueville's parents were imprisoned and escaped execution only through the fall of Robespierre. Alexis was born in July 1805. During the Bourbon restoration, Alexis's father, Comte Hervé de Tocqueville, served as a government administrator.[2]

Tocqueville acquired through his upbringing a sense of nobility. The Revolution eliminated the formal noble class in one stroke, but it could not so easily eliminate the aristocratic sensibility developed over centuries. Throughout his life, Tocqueville harbored a natural affinity for the unity of life and experience and the orderliness characteristic of the old regime, as well as the opportunity for cultural and personal excellence that, in his view, it had supported. Moreover, his sense of nobility embraced notions of public service and public morality. The popular term *noblesse oblige* trivializes these notions: in our age, in which the idea of equality is orthodox, the very notion of privilege, much less the notion that concern for the welfare of society rather than self-interest could guide the conduct of a person from a privileged class, is suspect. In Tocqueville's family and in Tocqueville's thought, however, the sense of citizenship, of duty to society and the exercise of public trust, was fundamental. Tocqueville's biographer has written:

> Comte Hervé's career was devoted to public service; on this he spent himself (and his wealth) freely. For his son, this was the true virtue, inherited from aristocratic times—without it, life was tainted with a kind of moral decay.
>
> . . . His love of the intellectual life, his requirement of himself that he express this intellectual life in the form of clear ideas and use these ideas to form rules by which to live—this was what Comte Hervé received from Malesherbes and passed on to his son. . . . [Tocqueville's] consciousness of his lineage evolved into his need for a more than ordinarily rigorous intellectual life and this in turn evolved into the recognition that he was thereby in a better position to exercise the public virtues. This ethic was the essence of what he inherited from his father. . . .
>
> . . . Although Alexis de Tocqueville experienced periods of lassitude when, with his invalid's sensitivity, he wanted to withdraw, he had only scorn for the selfish epicureanism that brings a man to shut himself up with his private pleasures, even legitimate ones, and live sheltered from the risks and turbulence of public life.[3]

The complement to Tocqueville's appreciation of the old order was his appreciation of the modern age. Indeed, his sense of the meaning of the old order only fully emerged upon his sudden realization of modernity. As a child, Tocqueville lived in the shelter of his family's aristocratic tendencies. Then, at age sixteen, he experienced a transformation of consciousness that embodied the social upheaval of the Revolution. He availed himself of his father's library, which contained some modern works, including those of Voltaire, Montesquieu, Rousseau, and other eighteenth-century French philosophers. The effect on Tocqueville of reading modern thinkers was, by his own description, revolutionary. He suffered a loss of religious conviction, and, in his phrase, an "all-embracing doubt" consumed him.[4] His reading catapulted him from a world of faith to a world of reason and rationality, from one of emotion to one of thought, from feeling to idea, comfort to agitation. It thrust him, irrevocably—just as the Revolution had thrust French society, irrevocably—into modernity, into the world of skepticism. Tocqueville perceived in the modern world the same fundamental condition he now perceived in himself—the lack of unity.

From 1823 to 1826, Tocqueville studied law in Paris. He was serving as a junior magistrate at the time of the July Revolution, which resulted not in a republic but another monarchy. The symbolism of this result— the pretense that the old order had a future—disturbed him. The question for Tocqueville was not whether to resist the modern age and the forces of liberalism within his country. He understood that the notions of equality and representative government, having gotten loose, had destroyed the old order once and for all. The question, then, was how best to structure a democratic society: how to restrain the forces of disorder and immorality that democracy entertains—materialism, selfishness, license, the impulse to tyranny, individualism. Tocqueville thus accepted the terms of his "all-embracing doubt," disquieting though they were. He set out to apply reason and to determine the principles and charac-teristics of a stable and moral democratic society. Toward this end, he traveled to the United States. He and his friend and peer Gustave de Beaumont obtained orders from the French government to produce a report on the U.S. prison system, which they did,[5] but Toc-queville took the opportunity to study the whole of American society.

Tocqueville and Beaumont arrived in New York City on May 11, 1831. They traveled in a rough figure eight through upstate New York, Michigan, Montreal, Quebec, Boston, and Philadelphia, down through the Ohio and Mississippi River valleys to New Orleans, across the South and up to Washington, D.C., then Bal-timore, and finally back to New York City. They departed for home on February 20, 1832.[6]

The America visited by Tocqueville and Beaumont was itself in a period of turbulence. The nation was spreading rapidly westward. Suffrage was expanding through the abolition of property and religious qualifications, and the number of popular elective offices was increasing. The economy was a boom-and-bust affair: bank failures and speculation in land and crops were commonplace. The North and the South were squaring off over the use of tariffs on imported goods. The institution of slavery was on the verge of becoming a divisive national issue.

The president in the years 1831 and 1832, Andrew Jackson, was himself a source of tumult. Jackson's polit-ical affinities generally lay with the South and the West, but his surest political allegiance lay with what he per-ceived as the interests of the Union—the United States as a nation. He took office as a symbol of the "common man" but was by no means ordinary. Even before serving as president, Jackson had led a remarkable and controversial public life in politics and the military.[7] Jackson had lost the presidential election of 1824. He had won the popular vote and had led the other candidates in electoral college votes but had lacked the requisite majority in the electoral college to be declared the winner. In the ensuing House of Representatives vote, he had lost to John Quincy Adams. One of the other candidates, Henry Clay, had delivered House votes to Adams with the understanding that, in return, Adams would appoint Clay as secretary of state. The 1824 election immediately had become known as the "corrupt bargain."[8]

Jackson's election in 1828 was for many a triumph of democracy, for others a triumph of the vulgar, and his inauguration played to form. An unprecedented crowd of between fifteen and twenty thousand people descended upon Washington, D.C., for the inauguration. Immediately after administration of the oath of office on the East Portico of the Capitol, admirers broke through makeshift barriers and mobbed the new president. A swarm accompanied Jackson back to the White House for the inaugural reception, and he arrived to find a free-for-all in progress. The celebrants shattered china and glasses, soiled floors and furniture, overturned vessels of punch and liquor, and in their expression of ardor nearly suffocated their president. Removal of refreshments to an outside lawn was necessary to disperse the revelers.[9]

During two terms as president, Jackson regularly angered political opponents through his creative, expansive exercise of executive power. At one point, he prepared to use military force against South Carolina if the renegade state persisted in "nullification" of federal legislation. He prevailed in a bitter conflict over the country's banking system. He also prevailed in his long-term campaign to remove Indians from their traditional lands in the South. When he retired from office, he was both more beloved and more controversial than ever.[10]

In short, the America of the Jacksonian era was unrefined and confrontational. For Tocqueville, however, America was a subject of interest because its democratic experience was unadulterated—it had no history of aristocracy—and therefore it presented favorable conditions for an empirical study.

Democracy in America is a marvel, stunning in both ambition and execution. Tocqueville wrote the first volume in approximately a year's time. The second volume appeared in 1840, five years after the first. Tocqueville's method was classically objective. Employing basic tools of the social scientist—close personal observation, interviews, gathering of documentary material, critical review of the data, and force of intellect—he analyzed a functioning democratic society.

Tocqueville did not concern himself with pleasing anyone with *Democracy in America.* He did not seek to flatter Americans with respect to their political and social organization. He did not approach democracy, in its American form or more generally, as either an easily realized ideal or an abomination.[11] He sought to discern the elements essential to a stable, orderly, and moral democracy and thereby to encourage France to surrender the vestiges of the old order and to seek out new advantages in the modern world. Upon the publication of the first volume of *Democracy in America,* Tocqueville explained to a friend:

> To those for whom the word *democracy* is synonymous with destruction, anarchy, spoliation, and murder, I have tried to show that under a democra-

tic government the fortunes and the rights of society may be respected, liberty preserved, and religion honored; that though a republic may develop less than other governments some of the noblest powers of the human mind, it yet has a nobility of its own; and that after all it may be God's will to spread a moderate amount of happiness over all men, instead of heaping a large sum upon a few by allowing only a small portion to approach perfection. I attempted to prove to them that whatever their opinions might be, deliberation was no longer in their power; that society was tending every day more and more towards equality, and dragging them and everyone else along with it; that the only choice lay between two inevitable evils; that the question had ceased to be whether they would have an aristocracy or a democracy, and now lay between a democracy without poetry or elevation indeed, but with order and morality; and an undisciplined and depraved democracy, subject to sudden frenzies, or to a yoke heavier than any that has galled mankind since the fall of the Roman Empire.[12]

Tocqueville thus viewed American lawyers through the prism of American political organization. In his essay on lawyers in *Democracy in America,* he concluded that the legal profession is one of the essential elements of a stable and moral democracy. "The authority [Americans] have given to lawyers and the influence that they have allowed them to have in the government," Tocqueville began, "form the most powerful barrier today against the lapses of democracy"—against the "revolutionary spirit and unreflective passions of democracy."[13] The authority American society has given to lawyers, he perceived, is to conform social and political activity to law, and the influence it has allowed them is their pervasive presence in the formation, interpretation, and application of law. Like an aristocracy, lawyers have an "instinctive penchant for order" and a "natural love of forms," as well as a "great disgust for the actions of the multitude" and a secret "scorn [for] the government of the people."[14] Tocqueville reasoned that lawyers' natural inclination toward order and rules derives from their training, practices, and habits of mind—from their occupation. "They are masters of a necessary science, knowledge of which is not widespread; they serve as arbiters between citizens, and the habit of directing the blind passions of the litigants toward a goal gives them a certain scorn for the judgment of the crowd."[15] Unique qualities of American society also affect the outlook of its lawyers: "In America there are neither nobles nor men of letters, and the people distrust the rich. Lawyers therefore form the superior political class and the most intellectual portion of society." Such status, Tocqueville deduced, makes lawyers conservative as a social and political group, since structural change could only jeopardize their position.[16] Thus, "the more one reflects on what takes place in the United States, the more one feels convinced that the body of lawyers forms the most powerful and so to speak the lone counterweight to democracy in this country."[17]

Tocqueville perceived further, however, the American lawyer's utter dependence on the social and political foundations of his privilege and the objects of his superior outlook. He observed, for example, that although lawyers in America incline toward privilege they are obliged to attend to the demands of the people. This obligation, unlike that of the nobility in the old order, is not a matter of grace, honor, and public morality but of

occupational and political necessity. He observed that
although American lawyers are conservative, they are
extraordinarily adaptable, ever poised to shift allegiance.
Also, Tocqueville saw, again ironically, that the privilege that American democracy extends to lawyers contains the license to bring about democracy's undoing. He
observes that although lawyers' special authority
depends on American democracy itself, they have the
capacity, by way of their skills and their position, to corrupt the institutions and processes of democracy to serve
their own interests. In short, Tocqueville perceived the
fundamental, multiple dualities in the American
lawyer's character.

In perceiving lawyers as a unique social group with a
special political function in American life, locating the
roots of that uniqueness in their occupational training
and experience and the uses of that training in a democracy, and eliciting the duality of their nature, Tocqueville provided the foundation for our understanding
of American lawyers. His analysis endures because it is so
incisive.

Within a few years of Tocqueville's visit, the same
spirit that had landed Jackson in the office of the president all but destroyed the legal profession. In the middle
decades of the nineteenth century, popular antipathy
toward privilege did not spare the practice of law. State
legislatures, especially in the South and West, substan-
tially reduced or eliminated educational and profes-
sional-training requirements for admission to practice,
and opposition to any sort of organized bar was strong.[18]

About that same time, the Jacksonian age began to
yield to the age of industrialization. For the balance of
the nineteenth century and into the next, technological
developments transformed manufacturing, transporta-

tion, and communication, which in turn transformed social relationships, the scale and complexity of the economy, and the political structure. When Tocqueville toured the country, the frontier generally lay along the Mississippi River. The country continued to move west, and before the end of the century its final outlines had taken shape. Texas, California, Oregon, and Washington, for example, became states in 1845, 1850, 1859, and 1889, respectively. The Civil War nearly split the country in two, but the union held. Also, even as the country was expanding, the East and West Coasts were coming together. The completion of the first transcontinental railroad graphically illustrated this process: telegraph wires broadcast to both coasts the driving of the spike that joined the Central Pacific Railroad with the Union Pacific in Promontory, Utah, on May 10, 1869.[19]

The legal historian James Willard Hurst has identified 1870 as the year that roughly marks a major shift in the nature of American legal practice.[20] At that time, the profession began to recover its identity as a profession. For example, lawyers began to develop formal standards of practice and to establish bar associations to improve the public image of lawyers as a professional group. The first modern bar association, the Association of the Bar of the City of New York, formed in 1870, and the American Bar Association formed in 1878.[21] American lawyers also began to become self-conscious as an occupational group, and the literature of American legal practice began to flourish. Approximately by 1870, the processes and effects of industrialization and the rise of mass society overtook legal practice, as they overtook every other social institution. The major resulting processes and conditions of American legal practice are fragmentation of the bar, an ongoing crisis of profes-

sional conscience, specialization of practice, and diversification of the lawyer's craft.

Fragmentation of the bar involves the gravitation of
different portions of the bar toward different societal
interests. This fragmentation is informal and multidi-
mensional. The fragments of the bar do not have sharp
boundaries and do interact with each other, but they
operate as separate worlds rather than as various functions of a unified whole. Many cluster around a specialization of practice, the most extreme example of which is
the patent bar, which has its own examination for admission to practice. Others cluster around a type of client,
still others around the common sympathies of the
lawyers involved. Most involve a combination of factors.

The first to notice the earliest, rough division within
the American bar was Lord Bryce. Born in 1838 into a
Presbyterian, scholarly Scottish family and educated at
Oxford, James Bryce became a man of wide learning,
especially in history, politics, literature, and law. When
Bryce's *American Commonwealth* was first published in
1888, Bryce held a chair in law at Oxford, was a member
of the House of Commons, and was an experienced trav-
eler in the United States. Bryce seems never to have met
an American of any class or creed with whom he did not
want to converse, but his learning and connections provided unusual access to the well-to-do and men and
women of public affairs. In 1870, on his first trip, for
example, Bryce struck up friendships with Julia Ward
Howe, Henry Wadsworth Longfellow, Oliver Wendell
Holmes Jr., James Russell Lowell, Ralph Waldo Emer-
son, Charles W. Eliot, and John Murray Forbes. On his
third trip to the United States, in 1883, Bryce conducted
a graduate seminar on *Democracy in America* at Johns
Hopkins University. Bryce expressed admiration for

Tocqueville's work but meticulously pointed out predictions that had proven erroneous, and he disputed Tocqueville on numerous points. Bryce's fascination with the United States, awareness of changes wrought by industrialization and the Civil War, and dissatisfaction with antiquated and patronizing views of the United States prevalent among the British at the time compelled him to compose a thorough, contemporary assessment of American society.[22] Like Tocqueville, Bryce relied on personal observation, a wealth of personal conversations with countless Americans, correspondence, and stores of government publications, newspapers, and other primary data. His *American Commonwealth* focuses largely on the workings of American politics in the late nineteenth century, but it also considers social and economic institutions such as the legal profession. His assessment of American lawyers[23] addressed Tocqueville on several points, most notably in the estimation that lawyers no longer exerted as much of a restraining influence on the forces of excess within American democracy as in the past.[24] Bryce also observed casually that some lawyers were tending largely or exclusively toward courtroom-related work, others toward business-related, noncourtroom work.

The main force that drew some lawyers away from the courtroom toward the office was the corporation. Lawyers long had provided counsel to corporations, but, by the late nineteenth century, when corporations collectively were becoming a major economic force, a portion of the bar formed an attachment to them. Moreover, as Louis Brandeis indicated in a speech at Harvard University in 1905, the portion of the bar devoting its services to the interests of corporations tended to be the most capable lawyers in the profession.[25]

At this early stage, the process of fragmentation entwines with another condition of the modern legal profession, its crisis of conscience. Bryce noted the rumor that corporations were corrupting the bar. Brandeis presented the rumor as an accomplished fact, charging that lawyers had become servants of large private business interests and had neglected "the people"—had abandoned their role as a "brake" on democracy. He chastised lawyers for taking legal positions on behalf of corporate clients that they would oppose privately. Five years later, in a speech to the American Bar Association, Woodrow Wilson berated the legal profession for abdicating its public responsibility, citing service to corporate interests as a primary example.[26]

Brandeis, Wilson, and similar critics appropriated Tocqueville's conclusion that the lawyer is crucial to the success of American democracy, but they ignored the considerations on which Tocqueville based that conclusion—the lawyer's education and training and the nature of the lawyer's work. They narrowed the role of the lawyer to a particular obligation—in Brandeis's words, "the obligation to use [his] powers for the protection of the people,"[27] meaning not to use those powers to protect the interests of the wealthy and the corporation. The claim has political benefits, but it is not entirely cynical. Nevertheless, the claim has become the reality. The belief that lawyers have this special obligation to the American public has become part of the occupational ideology of the American lawyer. The concern that the legal profession is failing to meet this obligation remains with the profession to this day.[28] It manifests itself, in part, as a contributing factor in the continuous fragmentation of the bar.

The early gravitation of a portion of the bar toward

corporate interests had a counterpart, the gravitation of another portion toward the interests of the poor. Industrialization resulted in a large urban working class, much of which was unskilled and poor, with little prospect for a better life. Beginning in the late nineteenth century, partly out of recognition of a new interest, partly out of the sense of professional obligation, and partly out of personal interest, a small number of lawyers made the concerns of the poor the focus of their work.[29] From the start, the portion of the bar that has worked for corporate interests and the portion that has worked for the poor have had little to do with each other.[30]

The rise of large-scale regulatory and administrative government through the Depression and the Second World War facilitated further fragmentation. The growth of a massive administrative apparatus to formulate government policy and to implement it created new interests, including the interest of the government itself. The new and expanding administrative departments provided new career opportunities for lawyers and also appeared to present a new means to serve the public.[31] Private interests needed lawyers, too, to represent them through administrative processes. The symbiotic world of government lawyers addressing the conduct of private interests and private lawyers addressing government administration developed as a result.[32]

The gravitation of a portion of the bar toward government-related work had a counterpart. By the mid-1960s, the criticism that the government no longer represented the public—that it represented, instead, the interests of big business and other forces it was supposed to control—became commonplace.[33] Some lawyers who shared this perception set out to represent what they considered to be the unrepresented public. These lawyers called themselves "public interest lawyers." The identity of the public that public interest lawyers represent, however, is debatable.[34] In practice, "public interest" is a euphemism for specialized political interest. Since the early 1970s, the institutionalized practice of public interest law has expanded to include all manner of political interests, from consumer and environmental protection to advocacy of abortion rights and the so-called neoconservative agenda.

The fragmentation sketched here relates to the two major structural transformations in American society during the past two centuries—industrialization and the rise of large-scale bureaucratic government. Fragmentation continues throughout the bar and now has a generational aspect. Recently, for example, the "cause lawyer" has emerged. Cause lawyers represent a breaking-off from not only the traditional bar but also previously established fragments such as poverty lawyers and public interest lawyers. Cause lawyering, according to its chroniclers, is a global rather than purely American phenomenon and is "everywhere a deviant strain within the legal profession." Cause lawyering is different, its chroniclers say, because it "gives priority to political ideology, public policy, and moral commitment." Cause lawyers are "moral activists" who "commit themselves and their legal skills to furthering a vision of the good society" and thus "help legitimate the legal profession as a whole." At the same time, they "threaten the profession by destabilizing the dominant understanding of lawyering as properly wedded to moral neutrality and technical competence."[35] Cause lawyers are only one of countless varieties of subspecies across today's bar.

The specialization that occurs in individual law practice is the corollary to the fragmentation of the bar as an occupational group. Specialization of legal practice involves, variously, the development of expertise in a particular area of law, or representation of a particular type of client. As society becomes more complex, the law becomes more complex, and the needs of clients and types of clients multiply and diversify. By the early twentieth century, an individual lawyer could neither master all of law and all forms of practice nor respond to a variety of problems with the efficiency and expertise demanded by clients. Since that time, new varieties of social activity have generated immeasurable expansion in substantive law, procedures, and administrative regulations. Furthermore, specialization reinforces specialization: a lawyer's development of expertise in a particular area attracts more clients for that expertise, which produces still more depth of expertise, still more clients, and so on.

The rough division within the bar between courtroom and business lawyers that Lord Bryce observed was early fragmentation based on early specialization. Further specialization soon followed. The rise of corporations that first diverted lawyers from the courtroom into office practice led to specialization within corporate law practice. Corporations—complex business organizations—invariably require at any given time a variety of legal services. No single lawyer could acquire and maintain thorough, current knowledge regarding all legal contingencies affecting the business of corporations. The law firms with large corporation clients responded by developing in each of its attorneys a particular area of expertise—one attorney or small group of attorneys handled tax problems, another handled employment and labor issues, another business contracts, and so on—so that collectively the firm could meet all the clients' needs. The rise of large-scale government administration added another dimension of legal complexity to corporate business, generating demand for still more varieties of expertise.[36]

Corporations were only the first type of client to need varied, specialized legal assistance. Since the mid–twentieth century, specialization at a basic level has been nearly universal: the lawyer tends to work in one substantive area of law or one style of practice. Thus, one is, for example, primarily or exclusively a litigator, a business lawyer, a regulatory expert, a lobbyist, or a family-law practitioner. Over the course of a career, a lawyer gains experience and knowledge in areas outside his normal expertise and may move from one area of expertise to another. At any moment, however, one specialty tends to dominate the practice, and over the course of a career an individual lawyer never touches vast areas of law and procedure. The tendency, moreover, is toward ever more refined specialization. Increasingly the lawyer specializes, say, not simply in litigation but in construction litigation or environmental litigation or class actions, not simply in business law but in mergers and acquisitions, not simply in real estate but in development of strip mall shopping centers, or not simply in intellectual property but in property rights relating to information technology.

For the lawyer, one other consequence of industrialization and the rise of mass society has been the diversification of skills. Whether working on behalf of a corporation, the poor, a labor union, a minority group, a spouse seeking divorce and child custody, or any other type of client, lawyers exercise a variety of skills. Even in representing a single client in a single matter, the modern lawyer must be more versatile and more agile than his nineteenth-century ancestor. This change is somewhat a matter of form rather than substance. Even in the traditional role of representing a client in a lawsuit, the lawyer employs many skills—not only making legal arguments, but also gathering information, negotiating, and counseling, to name some broad categories. Since the late nineteenth century, however, these and others of the lawyer's skills have become more variegated, more fully formed. Some have become specialties in themselves.

The core of the lawyer's craft remains legal argumentation. This skill entails manipulating facts and legal authority, such as court decisions, statutes, and regulations, to construct a basis for reaching a particular outcome in a legal dispute. It underlies all of the lawyer's other skills.

In 1929 and 1930, Karl Llewellyn delivered to Columbia University law students a series of lectures subsequently published as *The Bramble Bush.* The centerpiece of the lectures was an exposition of the case system both as a method of study and as the means of common law adjudication. Llewellyn offered the students basic instruction on how to read cases—how to read the written decisions of the courts: He identified the "assumptions" or ground rules on which courts operate in deciding the case. He emphasized careful reading and the importance of understanding every word—not simply Latin phrases or legal terms, but everyday words as they are used in the decision. He paused to consider the mutually dependent processes of, on one hand, how to break down the case into component parts, such as the facts, the parties' separate arguments, the specific legal issue, the rule of law, the holding or decision, and the reasoning of the court, and, on the other, how to construct the meaning of the case. He stressed the necessity of reading a case in the context of related cases. He counseled distinguishing among the facts, the interpretation of the facts, and the rule of law set forth by the court. He suggested that the rule of the case according to the court may not be the "true" rule of the case—the rule that other courts apply based on the case. He called attention to the "attitude" of the court toward the issue decided, especially in relation to that of other courts. Finally, he turned to the notion of precedent—existing legal authority in the form of prior decisions on a question of law—and demonstrated how a prior decision may have more than one meaning when considered with respect to a new and different case.[37]

In instructing on how to read cases, Llewellyn happened also to instruct on how lawyers make a legal argument. As Llewellyn told his students, if one can read a case in all its complexity, its variable meaning, one then has "the tools for arguing from that case as counsel on *either* side of a new case."[38] The lawyer makes a legal argument in the same way that a court explains its decision: by manipulating facts, legal authorities, and the relationships between them. The lawyer making a legal argument emphasizes some facts more than others, promotes a particular interpretation of the facts, and urges application, modification, disregard, or reversal of existing legal authority—all in an effort to persuade the decision maker to make a particular decision in the new and different dispute at hand.

The diversification of the lawyer's skills beyond legal argumentation became fully apparent by the middle of the twentieth century. Lawyers had assumed such varied functions as creators of new forms and mechanisms of social activity ("social inventors," in Willard Hurst's phrase), experts in vast expanses of social activity ("masters of fact"), intervenors and tacticians in public and private business ("administrators of social relations"), and leaders in the formulation of the symbols that express American society's beliefs and the rituals employed to maintain those symbols ("symbol makers").[39]

Another skill or set of skills that lawyers had developed to a high degree by the mid–twentieth century was facility in government administration—essentially, expertise in navigation of bureaucracy. These skills were necessary not only for the government lawyer or administrator but also the lawyer who worked with the government, in some fashion, from the outside. Every lawyer in the United States must cultivate this skill to some degree. The outside lawyer needs expertise that matches that of the administrative agency with or against which he is working—expertise regarding the authority, procedures, and dynamics of the agency; the industries and activities affected by the agency; and the client's activities.[40]

Diversification of lawyers' skills, fragmentation of the bar, and specialization of practice continue in response to the ever-increasing complexity of mass society and in response to the American political structure's dependence on lawyers. The lawyer's basic, integral function in America has not changed since Tocqueville's time, while, given the changed conditions of American life since the mid–nineteenth century, the lawyer's presence and influence are more pervasive than ever.[41]

Lawyers embody the tensions within American society. These tensions take form as the dual nature of lawyers that Tocqueville perceived nearly two centuries ago. Lawyers, in their occupational character, are neither only conservative nor only progressive—they are both. They are neither only technicians, heads bent to intricacies of rules and procedures, nor only statesmen, looking out with a broad vision and bridging vast political and social gaps—they are both. Lawyers are both elitist and populist. They are self-interested but have an interest in the public welfare. This dual nature is essential to lawyers' function in American society.

Modern American society keeps the bar in disarray. It continually pushes and pulls the bar in new, far-flung, and conflicting directions. Fragmentation and specialization result in the accumulation of particularized knowledge within individual lawyers and groups of lawyers, but they also partition knowledge and expertise across the profession. The lawyer who knows how to draft a complaint tends to know nothing about drafting a securities registration statement or negotiating a collective bargaining agreement. Lawyers who have a working knowledge of the needs of the poor tend to have no working knowledge of the needs of a start-up company or a bank. Segregation of knowledge and experience does not mean that lawyers cannot do work outside the normal scope of their practice—rather, it means that as a practical matter they generally do not. Diversification of skills tends to dilute the definitive skill of lawyers, making legal arguments. The anxiety over the lawyer's perceived public obligation fosters antagonisms within the bar.

Modern society also helps to hold the bar together. America's political structure remains fundamentally unchanged since its inception, and it therefore continues to need a professional group with expertise in reconciling law to social activity. The constant increase in the complexity and pace of change increases the need. Also, the segregation and partitioning of knowledge creates intraprofessional dependence: when the lawyer encounters an area of law in which he has no experience and cannot efficiently become competent, he must consult a specialist in that area. Lawyers' dependence on each other fosters a sense of common professional identity.

Lawyers, for their part, incessantly churn the social order. In making a legal argument to a court, the lawyer asks the court to alter the law. The lawyer urges the application of an existing rule to a new and therefore different circumstance, the modification of an existing rule in light of the new circumstance, or the creation of a new rule altogether. In making a legal argument to a court, the lawyer disturbs the social order by demanding that the court consider the requested adjustment. The existing arrangement is under constant assault from all directions by countless legal arguments in countless cases every day. In making legal arguments in other arenas, outside of court—for example, in private negotiations, before administrators and regulatory boards, or before legislative committees—lawyers similarly upset the social order. The steady assault of legal arguments by lawyers keeps institutions from rest. Lawyers roil the social order even more obviously as social inventors; as masters of fact, in which they assemble and interpret information "as a prerequisite to effective action" in society, to use Hurst's words; as administrators of social relations, in which they act as advisers in government and private business; as symbol makers; and as agitators on both sides of government administration.

Lawyers also incessantly cement the social order. The lawyer binds disparate and competing interests to each other and to society through the institution of law. In making a legal argument, the lawyer transforms a raw, stray social interest into a refined legal claim, reconciling the interest and the law to each other. The lawyer represents the interest to the law and the law to the interest. The churning and cementing are one and the same.

In this churning and cementing the lawyer does not act of his own accord. Lawyers do not ply their trade willy-nilly. They do not choose the issues and conflicts, private and public, that arise. They also do not make the rules and decide the outcome of disputes. Lawyers are an independent group, distinct because of their particular knowledge and their privilege to practice law, yet they do not control society. Lawyers are agents of society. In making legal arguments and applying their other skills, lawyers serve society's basic process of tearing itself apart and putting itself back together simultaneously and continuously.

CHAPTER TWO

The Judicial Process

The parties that lawyers represent—say, a corporation, a government agency, a spouse, or a landlord—may be at a given time in conflict with other parties—another corporation, a private business, the other spouse, a tenant. The conflict is an indication of disorder. Moreover, the interests in which lawyers represent parties—the pursuit of money, of some new advantage, of some vision of the way things ought to be, or of some other satisfaction—if realized, change the social order in some way. Even pursuing such interests upsets the social order.

In the United States, the forum to which parties resort for resolution of conflict, for clarification of rights and responsibilities toward each other, is the courts. Private parties and the government bring conflicts to the courts in the form of lawsuits. The case or lawsuit frames the conflict as a legal issue or several legal issues. The court resolves the conflict by resolving the legal issues—by determining the facts and the applicable rules of law and then applying the rules to the facts. A rule of law is a standard of conduct or a formulation of a social relationship that carries the legitimate authority of the state. Either a judge or a jury, depending on the situation, determines facts, but only judges determine the rules that apply and how to apply them. With respect to a given legal issue or the entire case, the court issues a decision, often in written form. The decision announces the outcome and, typically, the reasons for it, including a statement of the facts, the legal issue or issues, and the applicable rules of law, as well as a discussion of the application of the rules to the facts.

The question of how judges decide cases and legal issues—how judges determine what rule to apply in a particular situation and how to apply it—has preoccupied lawyers, litigants, politicians, and other students of law for as long as courts have adjudicated disputes. William Blackstone's *Commentaries on the Laws of England,* first published in 1765 through 1769, popularized the understanding that the law preexists and judges find it. Blackstone's purposes in delivering the *Commentaries* included demonstrating the superiority of the common law to a civil code system and establishing the common law as a legitimate field of academic study. To this end, he promoted the view of the common law as a science.[1] This science is rational not in the sense of formal logic or of a superimposed order, but as an organic system developed through history. The common law does not engineer social life but grows out of it. Underlying the cryptic and rigid forms of pleading and the mass of accumulated court decisions, Blackstone explained, is an identifiable system of substantive rules, of "customs" and "maxims." The reason of the rules lies in their derivation—from social life itself. "But here," Blackstone observed, "a very natural, and very material, question arises: how are these customs or maxims to be known, and by whom is their validity to be determined? The answer is, by the judges in the several courts of justice. They are the depositaries of the law; the living oracles, who must decide in all cases of doubt, and who are bound by an oath to decide according to the law of the land."[2] Court decisions are not the law but are evidence of the law.[3] The judge cannot change the rules of law.

> For it is an established rule to abide by former precedents, where the same points come again in litigation: as well to keep the scale of justice even and steady, and not liable to waver with every new judge's opinion; as also because the law in that case being solemnly declared and determined, what before was uncertain, and perhaps indifferent, is now become a permanent rule, which it is not in the breast of any subsequent judge to alter or vary from, according to his private sentiments: he being sworn to determine, not according to his own private judgement, but according to the known laws and customs of the land; not delegated to pronounce a new law, but to maintain and expound the old one.[4]

If a prior judicial decision is "most evidently contrary to reason" or "clearly contrary to the divine law," then "the subsequent judges do not pretend to make a new law, but to vindicate the old one from misrepresentation. For if it be found that the former decision is manifestly absurd or unjust, it is declared, not that such a sentence was *bad law,* but that it was *not law;* that is, that it is not the established custom of the realm, as has been erroneously determined."[5] Every rule has a reason deeply rooted in history. "The doctrine of the law then is this: that precedents and rules must be followed, unless flatly absurd or unjust: for though their reason be not obvious at first view, yet we owe such a deference to former times

as not to suppose they acted wholly without consideration."[6] The law is infallible, but not the judge: "So that
the law, and the *opinion of the judge,* are not always con-
vertible terms, or one and the same thing; since it sometimes may happen that the judge may *mistake* the law."[7]

The United States developed a common law and a
system of adjudication influenced by, but not identical
to, the English common law and the English system. In
1871, Harvard Law School professor Christopher
Columbus Langdell reinvigorated the understanding of
the law as science. In the preface to a new casebook on
the law of contracts, Professor Langdell stated: "Law,
considered as a science, consists of certain principles or
doctrines."[8] Compared to Blackstone's, Langdell's use of
the term *science* inclines more toward taxonomy, less
toward a system growing out of the history of a society,
and Langdell did not address the question of how judges
decide cases.

> The number of fundamental legal doctrines is
> much less than is commonly supposed; the many
> different guises in which the same doctrine is con-
> stantly making its appearance, and the great extent
> to which legal treatises are a repetition of each
> other, being the cause of much misapprehension. If
> these doctrines could be so classified and arranged
> that each should be found in its proper place, and
> nowhere else, they would cease to be formidable
> from their number.[9]

Langdell's view of law as a science, however, accommo-
dated the Blackstonian notion that judges find the law.

In 1921, Benjamin N. Cardozo delivered a series of
four lectures subsequently published under the title *The*

Nature of the Judicial Process. At the time of the lectures, Cardozo served on the New York Court of Appeals. Because of the prevailing, Langdell-inspired understanding of the judge's craft, Cardozo's eloquent, frank, and scholarly discourse had the immediate effect of revelation, if not revolution.[10]

In introducing the lectures and framing the issue for discussion, Cardozo smuggled in his revelatory concept:

> What is it that I do when I decide a case? To what sources of information do I appeal for guidance? In what proportions do I permit them to contribute to the result? In what proportions ought they to contribute? If a precedent is applicable, when do I refuse to follow it? If no precedent is applicable, how do I reach the rule that will make a precedent for the future? If I am seeking logical consistency, the symmetry of the legal structure, how far shall I seek it? At what point shall the quest be halted by some discrepant custom, by some consideration of the social welfare, by my own or the common standards of justice and morals? Into that strange compound which is brewed daily in the caldron of the courts, all these ingredients enter in varying proportions. I am not concerned to inquire whether judges ought to be allowed to brew such a compound at all. I take judge-made law as one of the existing realities of life. There, before us, is the brew. Not a judge on the bench but has had a hand in the making.[11]

Cardozo appeared to be suggesting that judges *make* law. They do not channel it or uncover it: they create it. As if to compound the shock, Cardozo then suggested that they make law based on subjective judgment.

There is in each of us a stream of tendency . . .
which gives coherence and direction to thought and
action. Judges cannot escape that current any more
than other mortals. All their lives, forces which
they do not recognize and cannot name, have been
tugging at them—inherited instincts, traditional
beliefs, acquired convictions; and the resultant is an
outlook on life, a conception of social needs, a sense
in [William] James's phrase of "the total push and
pressure of the cosmos," which, when reasons are
nicely balanced, must determine where choice shall
fall. In this mental background every problem finds
its setting. We may try to see things as objectively
as we please. None the less, we can never see them
with any eyes except our own. To that test they are
all brought—a form of pleading or an act of parlia-
ment, the wrongs of paupers or the rights of
princes, a village ordinance or a nation's charter.[12]

This understanding—that judges actually make law and
that they do so on a subjective basis—still begs the question of how judges decide cases. It raises the problem of
how the judge exercises the freedom to make law, how
the judge's "stream of tendency" affects the decision.
Before proceeding, Cardozo expressly confined his discussion to the context of the common law—areas of law
developed by the courts in the absence of legislative or
constitutional pronouncements. He noted, however, that
"the work of a judge in interpreting and developing
[constitutions and statutes as sources of the law] has
indeed its problems and its difficulties, but they are
problems and difficulties not different in kind or measure from those besetting him in other fields."[13]

In the first two lectures, Cardozo identified four "methods" of judicial decision making—four "directive forces" or considerations. The first he called the "method of philosophy," by which he meant the use of logic or reasoning by analogy. The second he called the "method of evolution," by which he meant special attention to the historical origin and development of a rule of law. By the "method of tradition" he meant deference to the customs of the community. By the fourth, the "method of sociology," he meant concerns for "justice, morals, and social welfare, the *mores* of the day."[14] Cardozo elaborated:

> Social welfare is a broad term. I use it to cover many concepts more or less allied. It may mean what is commonly spoken of as public policy, the good of the collective body. In such cases, its demands are often those of mere expediency or prudence. It may mean on the other hand the social gain that is wrought by adherence to the standards of right conduct, which finds expression in the *mores* of the community. In such cases, its demands are those of religion or ethics or of the social sense of justice, whether formulated in creed or system, or immanent in the common mind. One does not readily find a single term to cover these and kindred aims which shade off into one another by imperceptible gradations.[15]

Under this last method, the judge focuses on the ends that the rule to be laid down will serve. The four methods overlap, Cardozo explained, and more than one may inform a decision. The last method, however, is paramount:

It is the arbiter between other methods, determining in the last analysis the choice of each, weighing their competing claims, setting bounds to their pretensions, balancing and moderating and harmonizing them all. Few rules in our time are so well established that they may not be called upon any day to justify their existence as means adapted to an end.[16]

Cardozo devoted his third lecture to the matter of the judge's freedom or "The Judge As a Legislator." In this lecture, he qualified his central observation that judges make law. He insisted that in most cases the judge actually has no freedom to create because, he said, in most cases "the law is so clear."[17] The freedom to make law only arises in the rare "gap" or "open space" or "waste space" of the legal landscape, where other cases have yet to tread. Still, he explicitly rejected the notion that the law preexists: "Within the confines of these open spaces and those of precedent and tradition, choice moves with a freedom which stamps its action as creative. The law which is the resulting product is not found, but made."[18] In expounding on the judge's freedom within the gaps in the law, Cardozo mingled the matter of how the judge does decide a case with the matter of how the judge should decide a case. He spoke repeatedly of the judge's duties—for example, the duty to strive to determine the social welfare objectively and the "duty, within the limits of [the judge's] power of innovation, to maintain a relation between law and morals, between the precepts of jurisprudence and those of reason and good conscience."[19] In deciding cases, Cardozo explained, judges must attend to these various duties to society.

In the final lecture, Cardozo first addressed the matter of precedent. He reminded his audience that in a common law system—a system in which rules of law are provided through the adjudication of discrete, individual disputes—the rule of law governing a particular situation only emerges after the fact.

> No doubt the ideal system, if it were attainable, would be a code at once so flexible and so minute, as to supply in advance for every conceivable situation the just and fitting rule. But life is too complex to bring the attainment of this ideal within the compass of human powers.[20]

Thus the judge provides the rule and its application after the social activity has occurred, after the conflict has taken shape. Cardozo observed further that, as his audience well knew, in common law adjudication a decision has not only this "retrospective effect" but also prospective or precedential effect. The notion of precedent discussed by Cardozo is that a rule of law, once laid down, should be followed in similar situations in the future. Cardozo noted a tension between the need for uniformity and certainty (which, like Blackstone and others, he associated with adherence to precedent) and the need for justice. Cardozo did not advocate discarding adherence to precedent altogether, but he did say the practice should be "relaxed": "I think that when a rule, after it has been duly tested by experience, has been found to be inconsistent with the sense of justice or with the social welfare, there should be less hesitation in frank avowal and full abandonment."[21] Indeed, Cardozo suggested that rules of law are tentative and provisional.[22] In a set of follow-up lectures two years later, Cardozo stated the idea more directly. "Principles and precedents . . . are in truth provisional hypotheses, born in doubt and travail, expressing the adjustment which commended itself at the moment between competing possibilities. We need not wonder that there is disappointment, ending in rebellion, when the effort is made to deduce the absolute and eternal from premises which in their origin were relative and transitory."[23]

Cardozo concluded *The Nature of the Judicial Process* by reflecting on the human nature of judges. "Subconscious forces"—influences like circumstances of birth, education, occupation, and social circles—are always working on the judge as on everyone else. These forces limit the judge's ability to obtain a purely objective perspective and to make law that accords with, in Cardozo's phrase, "the aspirations and convictions and philosophies of the men and women of [the] time." In short, because judges are human, they make mistakes. He submitted, however, that "the endless process of testing and retesting" the law made by judges tends to correct mistakes over time.[24]

Thus, in the end, Cardozo never explained how a judge decides a case. Cardozo's suggestion that considerations relating to the social welfare are paramount means that this fourth method is the only method: the authority of either logic, historical development, or custom ultimately depends on whether the results produced square with the perceived best interest of society. This fourth directive force, however, does not prescribe how the judge determines what the rule will be or how to apply it. Considerations of social welfare leave the judge wide latitude to exercise creative freedom: for example, two different judges could have divergent opinions regarding the proper rule, or opposing views regarding a rule's application, and yet still claim the best interests of society.

Cardozo emphasized the judge's duties to society to discredit the notion that the judge's freedom to make law means that the judge operates under no constraints. The duties, however, are a matter of conscience and, even if the judge is conscientious, do not explain how the judge decides the case—how the judge determines the right rule and the right application. On that question, Cardozo said, "If you ask me how [the judge] is to know when one [social] interest outweighs another, I can only answer that he must get his knowledge just as the legislator gets it, from experience and study and reflection; in brief, from life itself."[25] This is both the only answer and no answer at all.

Nevertheless, the revelatory effect of the lectures— the understanding that judges make law and that they do so subjectively—endures. Since the time of the lectures, judges have been more forthcoming in discussing their work, but the understanding of how judges decide cases has not advanced beyond Cardozo's analysis.[26]

The shortcoming of the lectures is that Cardozo did not carry the understanding far enough. Contrary to Cardozo's assertion that judges make law only in the rare case, judges make law in every case. Even in announcing a decision in an area where the law is "clear," even in upholding an existing rule by applying it to a new case—even in "adhering to precedent," as Cardozo used the phrase—judges make law. Early in the lectures, speaking of the creation of a rule of law, Cardozo observed: "Until the sentence [the rule] was pronounced, it was as yet in equilibrium. Its form and content were uncertain. Any one of many principles might lay hold of it and shape it."[27] This observation holds true in every case. A rule of law derives meaning from its application to facts. No two cases are alike. To apply an existing rule to a later case is to change the rule. The meaning of a rule of law is clear only in the case in which it already has been applied. From one case to the next, the statement of the rule may not change, but the rule has no legal meaning apart from its application to facts. With respect to future cases, as Cardozo himself observed, a rule of law is a provisional hypothesis. It represents, as he said, the adjustment that seemed best to the judge at the time it was made under the circumstances of that case. The new case presents a different circumstance from the old case, and applying an old rule in the new case is making law.

Judges make law in every case—even in cases in which the legal issue is governed by constitutional provision, legislative statute, or administrative regulations. Such rules are law in that the failure to heed these standards and instructions, based on legitimate authority, carries legal consequences. On matters addressed by constitution or statute, the recognized responsibility of the court is to implement the policy that underlies the rule, not to change it. One problem, however, as Felix Frankfurter observed in a 1947 speech,[28] is that statutory rules consist of words and are therefore ambiguous. Another problem, also noted by Frankfurter, is that statutes are crude instruments: the drafters of legislative rules cannot predict the disputes, in all their complexity, to which the statute may be applied. Constitutional principles and administrative regulations are subject to the same problems. In the early nineteenth century, the U.S. Supreme Court claimed for the judiciary the role of final interpreter of the Constitution,[29] and, although the claim is debatable, the other branches of government generally have acceded to it. State courts followed suit, with like results. As a practical matter, the courts are the final interpreters of statutes and regulations, too. Moreover, many statutes and regulations are codifications of specific court decisions or whole areas of law developed by the courts. In circular fashion, these statutes and regulations then return to the courts for further clarification and development.

With respect to the interpretation of statutes, Frankfurter spoke of duties and restraints. He insisted, for example, that the judge must work within the limits of the policy chosen by the legislature and that, though words are ambiguous, the court must not "do violence" to them. He insisted, moreover, not only that the court must not legislate, but also that statutory construction by a court, despite considerable freedom, is not legislating. The very premise of his speech, however, was that statutes are not self-explanatory. In the "battle" of social life, he noted, the principle or statutory rule is unclear. When a problem of statutory construction arrives in court, "damage has been done or exactions made, interests are divided, passions have been aroused, sides have been taken."[30] "In the end," Frankfurter observed, "language and external aids, each accorded the authority deserved in the circumstances, must be weighed in the balance of judicial judgment."[31] Frankfurter is correct— and, though he could not bring himself to say it, this is making law. Constitutional principles, statutory rules, and administrative regulations, like common law rules, have clear meaning only with respect to factual circumstances to which they have been applied. Prior to their specific application, their meaning is speculative.

In the aggregate, the result of the judicial process is a complex, improvised system of rules. The rules emerge only out of available materials, the disputes brought before the courts. The rules, moreover, are certain only with respect to specific, past disputes.

This improvised system, as Judge Learned Hand related in 1929, is not an expression of the common will, "if by common-will we mean the assent of a majority of men and women alive today." It is, he observed, a set of responses to those motivated enough to seek resolution to their conflicts. The rest of society does not necessarily agree with the results or even give them a thought.[32]

This system is also always under construction. Every court decision modifies the system. More decisions occur every day.

Legal disputes are a sign of social disorder: of instability; of dissatisfaction on the part of some element in society; of some ambition for other than what the current order—the jerry-rigged system of provisional hypotheses—provides. In resolving discrete legal disputes, courts restore order in orderly fashion. They reconcile the parties to each other and to society by providing a forum, by considering the positions of the parties, and by making an adjustment through the creation of a rule and the application of it. The judicial process, however, in individual cases and collectively, is also disorderly: it does not follow a master plan—it improvises a solution. Moreover, this restoration of order promotes disorder, because the adjustment changes social relationships. It creates new standards, new ambiguities, new dissatisfactions, and new ambitions, providing the conditions for new disputes.

PART TWO

*The Moral Consciousness
of the Litigator*

CHAPTER THREE

The Two Rules of Practice

One of the witticisms that circulate through the back hallways and private offices of litigation practice upends the standard notion of the lawyer-client relationship: "There are two rules of practice. The first rule is The Client Is the Enemy. The second rule is Don't Forget the First Rule." One litigator, when reminded of the Two Rules, remarked with laughter, "And there's actually rule number three, Remember the Rules."

Many lawyers recoil instinctively from the Two Rules. Lawyers depend on clients for livelihood and career. This dependence fosters a public face of support for the client. Any suggestion that the client is the enemy is counterintuitive, possibly sinister, and poses survival and public relations problems. Some lawyers internalize the dependence on the client and the requisite public face so completely that "The Client Is the Enemy" is unthinkable.

As businesses, law firms must institutionalize the requisite public face, and phenomena like seminars designed to cultivate favorable attitudes toward the client are common. One litigator recalled a series of such sessions at her first employer, a firm heavily invested in

biotech patent litigation, and touched on what she perceived as the motives underlying them:

> We all had to go to these seminars, where like
> "Client First," "Always Be Friendly with the
> Client." It was just basically all these seminars on
> how to kiss client ass. And the secretaries had to do
> it as well actually, to change their behavior and the
> way how they spoke with anyone on the phone.
> Because it could affect, you know, whether a client
> came into the firm. . . . I think that, especially in
> the biotech world, if you land one case, you auto-
> matically are getting a sixty million dollar case in
> the door. In [the city where the firm is located], at
> least at the time I was there, almost every single
> biotech case you landed was worth *a lot.* These
> places, they wouldn't even litigate it unless they
> thought there's a lot of money at stake. And it
> would be the major, central patent in [the client's]
> portfolio, and they would be bringing it out.
>
> And so, what was happening, I think, the firm
> was just really sensitive about continually putting
> their best foot forward and not losing any clients
> that the firm already had in its grasp, but at the
> same time not doing anything to alienate any possi-
> ble new clients. I think by having this mentality of
> always think, you know, always have clients—part
> of it is just the fact that firms needed to make more
> money. That ties in with billing, with increased
> billing, so the fact that people were a lot more
> aware of how they managed their cases, make sure
> that more money was made. And I think as times
> changed, especially as middle-sized firms kept on
> getting phased out in [that region], firms were

really worried that they weren't marketing enough and they weren't landing the big cases, which would also gain more press coverage. It was getting really competitive for business.

Resistance to the Two Rules, however, is not strictly a function of business and professional imperatives. Litigators take to heart their professional identity and take pride in helping clients.

I think of us as professionals. And counselors, in every sense of the word. Just like a psychologist or a therapist, or somebody in the clergy, or a doctor. A confidante. . . . I think of [clients] as my family, not as my enemy. They're people that are hiring me because they trust my judgment, and that's really what they're looking for. Somebody who has good judgment, who can help guide them through something where they sometimes have real serious problems.

Litigators are quick to point out that the client is the one at risk:

I think the only way you can survive and be a lawyer is to really understand that. Understand that ultimately it's the client's business, life, whatever it is, that's at stake, and that you may never completely understand the client's motives or incentives to do whatever it is the client wants to do. It's just something that you have to understand that's beyond your control and that things may get settled or not settled, contrary to what you think is the rational or logical thing to do, because of that.

If you can't accept that as a litigator, then you're just going to be miserable. 'Cause it's the very rare client that just cedes everything to the lawyer and lets the lawyer make all the decisions. It does not bother me, just as a general matter.

Moreover, litigators commonly develop respect and appreciation for their clients. In such instances, their sincerity is unmistakable:

I've probably found a greater number of times . . . where it's the opposite. Where my clients have been my most important ally in a lawsuit. Where the clients have provided a tremendous amount of logistical support, a tremendous amount of legal support, where the litigation process, whether it's a written motion or oral argument or trial, or what have you, is much better because the client has really gotten into the guts of the thing and helped me out. That does happen also. There have been many clients that have become personal friends, people whom I originally met as a client, and then I've gotten to know because I thought so much of them, and they were so helpful in the litigation process.

A friendly relationship may also happen to yield business returns:

I'd have to say that [the Two Rules are] the antithesis of how I treat my practice and my clients. Basically, I've been fortunate enough to build up a decent little stable of clients that I've represented for many years now, where every time

they get a litigation matter or every time they get
an environmental matter, my phone rings. And as
to all of those clients, first of all, I've developed
relationships with them that transcend the professional relationship. I socialize with them outside
the office; I consider myself to have a relationship
that—well, I'll repeat myself: the relationship tran-
scends the professional.

I like my clients to feel like, not only am I
their friend, but—I see the relationship as sort of
the *consiglière* relationship, like the Mafia had with
the attorney that is their adviser on all things. The
Italian term *consiglière* really describes my view of
what your relationship with your client should be.
An adviser and a counselor and a confidante. And I
want them to feel like they can pick up the phone
and call me even if it's a matter that hasn't come in
the door yet necessarily, and chat with me for five
or ten minutes without me necessarily opening the
matter and sending them a bill. . . . I mean, my
clients send me Christmas gifts. They take me out
to dinner and insist on picking up the tab. It's a
relationship where I recognize that the smartest
thing I can do is, one, create a lot of trust, and two,
help the client's business be successful.

Still, the Two Rules do not circulate simply for their
shock value. They refer, if obscurely and humorously, to
the truth about the relationship between the lawyer and
the client. The truth is that, inherent in the relationship,
there is a tension.

This truth is not simply a matter of the client making the lawyer's life miserable with demands that seem
whimsical if not absurd. Experiences like the Friday

afternoon phone call are common: the client requests some new memorandum or draft of some document "first thing Monday morning," the lawyer sacrifices the entire weekend to prepare the document and deliver it on time, and then the client ignores it for days or weeks. Some litigators are able to joke about having to keep the client happy.

> One of the things that I've constantly been amused by, and there are other lawyers that I've talked to who are also amused by this, is when you have law students coming in and you're interviewing, and they all of course, just the way we did, want to be able to ask intelligent questions. And one of the standard questions that always seems to be asked is, "When do I get client contact?" Once you've been out for ten years or five years or whatever, you understand that client contact is not some [*laughing*] paradise-like experience. There are plenty of headaches associated with it. [*Laughing.*] Probably you'd say [more senior lawyers] would like less client contact, whereas people who aren't [yet] lawyers want client contact. I always get a chuckle out of that. You get this young kid across [your desk] going, [*in dramatically sincere voice*] "And how soon will I get client contact?" [*Laughing.*] It's like, well, you want it now, you can have it.

The truth is not so much the conflict over fees, though that conflict can be severe. As one litigator observes:

> There is absolutely no question but that today there are many, many businessmen and general counsel

out there who feel it is perfectly legitimate, indeed praiseworthy, to one way or the other con or strong-arm their outside lawyer into providing legal services without paying for those services.

It is also not the fear that the client may turn around and sue the lawyer for malpractice, which does happen and is always kept quiet.

Furthermore, the truth of the Two Rules does not arise from mistakes or misunderstandings on the part of the client. Every litigator can cite instances in which the client has overlooked, ignored, or misunderstood its obligations in litigation, putting the lawyer in the awkward position of having to explain to opposing counsel (or, worse, to a judge) why something was not done properly. Some mistakes and misunderstandings occur because of the client's laziness, forgetfulness, or errors in judgment. Moreover, typically the client is not a lawyer and does not understand the rules of litigation or the consequences of mishaps and missteps.

> There have been times . . . where it has been a terrible battle with my own client, and it can be a variety of things, where the client has made my job far more difficult. It may be that my client has not told me the truth about something that turns out to be important. Sometimes clients don't deliberately lie, they just forget or figure it's not important or what have you, but sometimes you end up being stuck, because you've taken the client's word for something and it turns out not to be the case. Other times you get in trouble because the client will promise to do something, to help find some documents or what have you, and they don't do it.

Sometimes the client's behavior is stupefying. One attorney recalls:

> We represented a state government in litigation, and the central part of the litigation was the pricing of a natural resource. And the question was—we had received a discovery inquiry as to what information and calculations we had on those pricing calculations. I was dispatched to the state offices and talked to a number of people, and most crucially there was one person who everybody identified as the key person on these calculations. I got to him and asked him what he had, and he gave me a surprisingly modest amount of information, which we, I believe, then produced. I don't think we caught it originally. But I remember sitting in his office, which was just *surrounded* by—all the walls were covered with file cabinets. What we later learned was *all* those file cabinets had stuff of the sort we were looking for. But his understanding was it was confidential.

This attorney corrected the oversight upon discovering it and suffered nothing more serious than embarrassment. He also, like many litigators in such situations, faulted himself for not being clearer in communicating to the client's representative what had to be done. Such instances may lead the litigator to wonder whose side the client is on, but litigators generally accept inadvertencies and minor confusion as part of litigation. The sheer magnitude of most modern litigation makes mistakes likely.

> When I started practicing . . . I was working on a document production and I was afraid we were

screwing it up along the way and that I was going to screw something up and we weren't going to find documents or something. And one of the partners I worked with said, "In the history of big case litigation, nobody has ever done a document production that didn't get screwed up in some way. You're always going to find new files, you're always going to find a new person that no one thought of, someone's always going to, somewhere along the line, turn up a new box, or someone's going to remember a storage closet where somebody's going to find an index that nobody saw before. And you're going to have to produce documents again. And you may have to reopen depositions. It happens all the time. And that's not because anyone is not trying to play by the rules or hide evidence, but mistakes happen." And when you're talking about cases involving big companies where there may be one hundred or two hundred people who have knowledge of the lawsuit or facts dating back [ten or fifteen years], it's inevitable that things are going to slip through the cracks.

So, that stuff happens. I never think of that as the client being the enemy, I think of that as the client has lots and lots of things that they're trying to do, the lawsuits are very important to them, but, at the end of the day, for most people, lawsuits and litigation [are] an expense item on their balance sheet, on the income statement, and they're expenses. So they devote a lot of resources to it, and you go, and you ask, and you shake the trees, and you open drawers, but things slip through the cracks. I never think of it as the client being the enemy.

Finally, the truth of the Two Rules is not the result of the client's business interests outside the litigation. Litigators accept that business interests may dictate strategies and even a specific resolution to the litigation, even though, strictly in terms of the litigation, yielding to the business interests produces a disastrous result. The following explanations by three different litigators are typical:

- I've been working on a patent case, and the client has a business interest—they're getting sued for infringing a patent. They have a business interest they're trying to protect, and they're just desperate to settle the case and get a license so that they have freedom to operate in this area. I thought there's a price at which you should settle—there usually is—but they got interested in a much higher number than I thought was justified. They ended up settling for the higher number just because they were so bent on getting the situation resolved. To me it was even unpleasant—most of the time, you settle a case, and everybody is kind of happy and patting each other on the back, even with opposing counsel. I just didn't even like talking to opposing counsel, because I felt like we gave up way more than I thought was justified in the case. So that's a little frustrating, where maybe the lawyer's perspective on things is different than what the client's is, but part of our job is you've got to understand that ultimately it's the client's money and the client that's being represented in the process.

- You certainly do get situations where you believe that you're at a point in the litigation that, if you had the budget, there are things you would do to position the litigation and steps that you would take that you think will enhance your client's position and resolve the case more quickly in the client's favor. But what you bump up against, or what I've bumped up against on occasion, is that the client will say because of cash flow issues, and budgeting issues, they just can't afford to do it at the time. So, as far as their calendar is concerned, their fiscal years and their budgeting purposes, they'd rather spend less money on the litigation, and keep it at a kind of, at a low level, because they'll have a better cash flow situation in maybe six months or a year. Where, if they were to pay a settlement that's going to be richer at that point, that's OK with them, because it's OK for them to pay a million dollars in six months, but it ain't OK to be spending two hundred thousand dollars a month right now. So you certainly do get that sometimes. But again I don't think of that as the client being the enemy. The client has to run their business, and the litigation, as I said before, the litigation is one out of a billion things they're thinking about, and it's an expense item. And they're just trying to monitor it, like any other expense item.

- But there are many cases where a client may well say, for example, "I want to settle with the other side, and settle promptly, even if I have to pay way too much money. We're in the process of super-secret merger discussions, and I've got to get this litigation cleared off the books so that the accountants will give us a clean audit opinion." I've always been of the opinion that, as long as I'm advising the client about what the consequences are of things, that those kinds of decisions that are made apart from strict litigation are absolutely legitimate and sometimes are far more important than the litigation.

Client caprices and idiosyncrasies, disputes over fees, fear of malpractice suits, mistakes, the client's business concerns—all of these are sources of irritation for the litigator trying to represent the client in a lawsuit, but none of these really substantiates the Two Rules. Rather, the tension to which the Two Rules refer stems from the same interests that bring the litigator and client together in the first place: the litigator is a professional and a specialist in litigation, and the client is not. The litigator has particular knowledge, experience, expertise, and, presumably and most importantly, judgment regarding the litigation process. Those are the attributes for which the client hires the litigator and for which the litigator undertakes the representation. The litigator has a sense of the shape, size, and intensity of the case and of its place among countless other cases in the courts. The litigator has an informed idea of how best to conduct the litigation on behalf of the client: what legal positions to take, when to act and to what degree, what tools to use and how to use them. When the client's conduct within the litigation usurps the litigator's professional judgment or precludes the exercise of that judgment on behalf of the client, "The Client Is the Enemy" applies. In such instances, that is, the client is its own worst enemy.

I've passed on the [Two Rules] from time to time since it directs attention to the sometimes neglected issue of the divergence between the client's interests and the lawyer's interests. Some conflicts are very familiar, such as the inherent conflict in any billing arrangement. But what interests me are the more subtle conflicts which arise from the fact that the lawyer, to do his/her job, cannot simply be a mouthpiece for a client. The litigator's goals and the client's goals are not likely to be completely congruent. It is the tension between what the litigator has to do and what the client may want that gives rise to "The Client Is the Enemy." Certainly the litigator understands that the client is the ultimate authority on most issues. But the litigation process leaves lots of room for friction between the lawyer and client. . . .

So, to summarize, everyone understands that the client isn't really the enemy. But the [witticism] highlights that the litigator needs to keep some distance and objectivity in order to serve the client effectively. From time to time that causes friction, but that is just part of the job. (If you only told clients what they wanted to hear, they could pay someone a lot less for the same result. And some clients choose to do that, and generally get what they pay for.)

The meaning of the Two Rules is not literal. Rather, they serve as a reminder that the professional is independent from the client.

Some litigators who recognize that the Two Rules refer to the tension inherent in the relationship still hear them too literally.

I don't think I've ever really felt [the Two Rules] had any particular accuracy for me. There's a sense

> that you have to work with your client sometimes
> because their desires whether emotional or busi-
> ness-driven don't necessarily stand in good stead
> legally, but I always think of that as more of a com-
> munication issue than finding them to be your
> enemy. There's a tension there, but it seems to me
> it's one to work through as opposed to fighting
> your client on it.

This point is well taken. Certainly, good communication
and willingness to understand both ends of the attorney-
client relationship may prevent the tension from becoming a problem. The same litigator comments further:

> There's something . . . really kind of arrogant about
> [the Two Rules] . . . this idea that, if they would
> just leave you alone and let you litigate away,
> everything would be fine. That the uninvolved
> client, the one who simply gives you carte blanche
> to make decisions to write the brief and to decide
> which procedural steps to take and when, and how
> to present them et cetera, is the best client. And it's
> when the client starts to become involved that they
> become your enemy because they're getting in the
> way of your unilateral decision making. I don't
> think it's wholly arrogant, but there's definitely
> something about that—it's akin to a doctor seeing
> a patient as antagonistic, because the patient is ask-
> ing a lot of questions about his or her health and
> what the best options are. Where the doctor would
> like to just go ahead and amputate. [*Laughing.*]

This doctor-patient scenario, however, is not directly
analogous to the Two Rules scenario. A more direct anal-

ogy would be a situation in which the doctor, trained to consider all treatment options and to promote the patient's overall health and to preserve the patient's life, concludes that amputation is the best course, but the patient insists on another course or takes some action, like handcuffing the doctor, so that the doctor cannot perform the operation properly. There, the patient is the enemy, so to speak. The truth of the Two Rules is not that the litigator should be free to act without reference to the interests of the client, that the best client is a headless client, or that the client should not ask questions. Indeed, the litigator has affirmative ethical duties under rules of professional conduct to keep the client informed and to abide by client decisions regarding the objectives of the representation. Rather, the truth of the Two Rules is that even in a litigator-client relationship that functions well, there is an inherent tension between the desires and interests of the client and those of the litigator working on behalf of the client.

One way the tension surfaces is insistence by the client on a particular course for emotional reasons. The litigator understands that clients and client representatives have emotions, but he knows that the litigation process is, ultimately, relentlessly rational.

> Well, sure, there are certainly situations when I
> have thought that a client wasn't really acting in its
> best interests. For instance, I might say—this actu-
> ally works both ways—I might be sitting there
> thinking, you know, this is a great time to settle
> this case, you're going to have some problems
> before a jury on this case, and you really ought to—
> it's not going to get better for you, it's going to get
> worse, and you really ought to negotiate a settle-

ment right now. Only to have the client say, no, I feel really good about this case, I think we're going to win, and I don't want to settle with this person at all. Or maybe just having an emotional reaction: I hate those people, I could never settle with them. Clearly there are situations like that, where the lawyer views him- or herself as the dispassionate individual who can analyze the situation and know what's right, and on the other hand you have a client who's more emotionally invested, and you don't agree with what the client's decision is, but you have to go along with it because, you know, they're the client.

Clients also get greedy. One litigator who likes to caution his clients, "Pigs get fat, hogs get slaughtered," relates this tale:

I was involved in a piece of litigation where I got summary judgment in some underlying matters, and then the opposing side did something else where I had to go into a different court. We had already won the important thing, I had already got-ten summary judgment against the other side. But the client decided that they wanted to go even fur-ther, and not just get 99 percent from the other side, they wanted to get 100 percent. So they wanted me to go into this other court and try to get the last 1 percent. I advised them that going into the other court would be risky and that chances are we would not prevail. But because we had been so successful in the major part of the case, the client got perhaps sold on the position too strongly.

We went into the other court and got killed. It was one of the worst courtroom experiences in my life. I felt so badly because I had put in a huge amount of work, and billed the client a huge amount, and the client paid it all, but it was frustrating to have been able to very clearly predict what was going to happen and to have explained the risks, and turn out to be right, and none of it made any difference because the client was being just too headstrong about something. It just was a very frustrating experience. Again, it's not because the client was evil, but they weren't getting the full value of my experience, my judgment, and as a result they ended up wasting a fair amount of time and money when they really didn't have to. It's that sort of thing that is really frustrating to me.

Some clients insist on micromanaging the case. This practice increases during economic downturns. It is almost certain to prove the truth of the Two Rules.

While client involvement is helpful in moderation, clients who want to decide on strategy and tactics, and clients who want to rewrite briefs do not advance their cases. (They also tend to be the clients who complain about their bills, which they have inflated by their micromanagement.) The point is simply that the client has to stand back to some extent to let the litigator conduct the litigation. The litigator is obligated to keep the client informed and to be sure that the overall direction is what the client wants. But issues like whom to depose and when must be decided by the lawyer, after hearing the client's views. When that necessary deference is lacking, "The Client Is the Enemy" comes to mind.

Micromanaging may take the form of dictating how the firm must staff the case—how many attorneys must be assigned to the case and their levels of experience as well as which attorneys must perform what tasks. It very likely involves budgeting—imposing a gross dollar cap on all litigation fees and expenses and particular dollar limits on different categories of tasks and stages of the litigation. It may involve dictating that a certain motion be filed and when that motion must be filed, or, as noted in the preceding quotation, whom to depose and when. It may involve rewriting briefs to be filed in court or insisting certain arguments be made in certain motions. The problem of the client's insistence on making certain arguments or telling certain stories in inappropriate situations is, as one litigator notes, "not so much that it's damaging" but that "it's not helpful . . . which is a more subtle thing." He elaborates:

> [The problem] is very common, not just procedural issues but can't we also make this argument, can't we also make that argument. And the answer often is, well, yeah, I suppose you could, but it's not a very good argument and it's going to get in the way. I think a very common misunderstanding for clients is to forget that their case, which to them is all-consuming and all-important, is just a wink of an eye in a judge's calendar. And this motion that you're bringing—to compel discovery responses or something—doesn't need to have a complete recapitulation of all the wrongs and the background

and everything else and the bad things the other side did, because the judge understands and you as a litigator understand that the only issue the judge has the slightest interest in is how to resolve this discovery dispute. . . . The client sometimes I think feels that you're not putting forth all the arguments that need to be put forward, but in fact you're just being slightly selective. That's very common—why aren't you including this, why aren't you including that—and the answer is that's not what this particular either motion or proceeding is about.

Micromanagement may take any number of other forms. Total micromanagement is rare; more typically, clients scrutinize or limit selected aspects of the litigation.

Micromanagement tends to hinder the litigator in the effort to help the client reach a favorable outcome in the litigation by artificially limiting the exercise of judgment and the ability to respond to changing circumstances—a constant of litigation. For example, imposing a strict budget may make sense to a businessperson but does not to anyone who understands the variables and vagaries of the litigation process. One never knows how obstreperous or unscrupulous or lazy or tenacious an opposing party or opposing counsel may be, how many witnesses may turn up, how many documents may have to be reviewed and organized, how many motions and what kinds will have to be filed or defended against, how much discovery the judge will allow, how the judge will rule on this or that motion, how receptive the judge may be to a novel legal theory, and so on, ad infinitum.

The client that is an organization may, by its very nature as an organization, undermine the litigator's efforts to assist the client. The organization is a single entity in the eyes of the law, as a party in the litigation, and as the client whom the attorney represents. The organization acts, however, through individuals, and individuals have interests that may be in conflict with the interests of other individuals and with the interests of the organization. Behavior that may make sense according to the logic of the organization is often counterproductive to the litigation.

> When an organization is the client, there are the competing interests of individuals in the organization. Employee A may be much more interested in causing Employee B to look bad than in winning the case for their common employer. And the employer can often be counted on to louse things up by firing for unrelated reasons the very employee who is needed to provide crucial evidence in the case.

Such internal problems tend to flare up when least convenient—when action must be taken. In-house counsel may only compound the problems that organizational dynamics present to the litigator. In-house counsel, because they are in-house—that is, within the organization—are as susceptible as nonlawyers to compulsions to not expose themselves, to defeat rivals, to secure or to advance their positions, and to push their own causes and ideas.

> Lots of these clients have in-house attorneys, some of whom have significant litigation experience— some of whom have *none,* of course. [*Laughing.*] I can recall the single most frustrating episode of exactly this sort, where we were doing a discovery

motion, trying to limit discovery, and the client
wanted to tell this enormously complex story, and
it was totally inappropriate. We had to go through
multiple declarations. At the last second, one of the
senior executives backed out and didn't want to
make a declaration, just because he didn't want to
attest to anything. I had two in-house attorneys
giving me edits that were contradictory. And the
CEO, who decided he didn't want to attest anymore. It was unbelievable . . . hellish . . . and the
worst offenders were trained attorneys, at least one
of whom was a litigator who practiced serious corporate litigation for eight or ten years.

Sometimes, the client disregards the litigator's professional skills and advice with such aplomb that even
those who are inclined not to think of the client as the
enemy, even in jest, must take notice. Such episodes
demonstrate that in rare instances the truth of the Two
Rules may indeed be literal.

I took a case to trial about three or four years ago,
and if I remember correctly it was one of the first
cases that I first-chaired all the way to jury verdict.
. . . [My client] was suing a seller of property for
breach of the sales agreement. And he truly
believed that he was smarter than everybody else
involved in the case. Smarter than me, smarter than
the opposing lawyers, smarter than the opposing
client, certainly smarter than the jury, and smarter
than the judge. And he thought that the *best* way to
win the case was for *him* to win the case. . . . The
thing is, what he was going to do is just exaggerate
the facts just slightly. Just a *little* exaggeration here

and there just to get the point across. We had what
I considered to be a very good case. And I knew
what I was dealing with with this client, because I
had already defended several, several days of his
deposition. Maybe a week or more of his deposition. And I knew of his propensity to try to help.
And I had pulled him aside on more than one occasion, and I had said, *"Really.* We have a good case.
We don't need any additional help."

   Well, sure enough, we got into trial, and he
got up on the stand. And decided to help. And surprised me by telling me things I didn't know—and
didn't believe. And sure enough, got his ass kicked
on cross. And we did everything we could to put
the case back together. It was a monthlong trial.
Monthlong trial. And he had testified, as you
might imagine, very early in the case. And sure
enough, we came to verdict—and this was a case
where the other side was one of those carpet-bomb
law firms. And they brought at least twenty summary judgment motions and motions *in limine.* Not
twenty separate motions, but they'd bring a motion
with five separate grounds for summary judgment,
five separate motions *in limine.* At least twenty of
'em. And we won every single one. *Every single one.*
We won every single pretrial motion and trial
motion. And I remember riding up the escalator in
the superior court building . . . and they were on
the escalator in front of me, a few steps in front of
me, and we were all smiles 'cause we had just *killed*
them in the last of these pretrial hearings. And they
were just *steaming,* and they turned back and said,
"Don't look so smug, we're going to appeal this
thing." We weren't even presenting evidence yet!

We hadn't even opened the trial, and they were already saying [they were] going to appeal it because of the judge's rulings on the summary judgment motions and motions *in limine.*

So, lo and behold, we come to the day the verdict is being read, and we're *defensed* [i.e., the jury finds in favor of the defendant on every issue]. And I am absolutely—I'm mortified. I cannot believe what's happened. And we go out into the hallway, and the jury is all out there, and now we're free to talk to the jury, and with my client in earshot, I walked up to the jury foreman and I said, "What happened? It seemed so *clear* that we had been injured. And that the defendant had breached the contract. What happened?" "We think your client's a liar. We thought you were a really good lawyer, better than the other side. We think your client's a liar. We just didn't believe him." And while the jury was deliberating, they [had] asked for part of the transcript to be read back to them, one part: a portion of his cross-examination where the opposing counsel was catching him in a lie. And that was it. The case—we had worked on this case for two years. It was a contingency fee case. We probably had somewhere between five and seven hundred thousand dollars' worth of attorney time into this case, and we walked away empty-handed because the client thought he was smarter than everybody else, ignored all of my warnings, and tried to help on the stand.

The litigation process is fertile ground for irony and, indeed, abounds with it. Specific actions taken by a party or by an attorney, the invocation or application of a rule, a court order or judgment, and random occurrences—such events change the stature and power of participants and create new relationships among them. This new landscape causes, in turn, new and unanticipated behavior. Even the Two Rules are subject to ironic consequences. Conduct by the client that defies the litigator's advice and destroys the litigator's effort to position the client favorably may have salutary results. Sometimes, that is, the client who is the enemy turns out to be the ally:

> [*Laughing.*] [I worked on] a case in which a former consultant of a company sued to obtain stock options he said he was owed. This was of course [a few years ago], when those kinds of things were much more highly valued. The company was doing very, very, very well. People who had been early employees and stuck around and not gotten into a fight with the founder were living very high on the hog. So, everybody who ever delivered pizza to the company suddenly came out and said they had options. And this guy was one of them. He had a contract that was a horrific construction by somebody who wasn't a lawyer, and it was ambiguous and it was harmful in the sense that it didn't explain in any way what the options were going to be or how they were going to vest or anything like that. And then the plaintiff consultant had really not done whatever work he was supposed to do. It was unclear that he'd done *anything* productive. And his total commitment to the company was, like, sixty hours or something.
>
> Anyway, the deponent was the founder of the company, and he was a named defendant and he

was clearly the main witness. And he was completely irritated by the fact that he was having to deal with this suit and having to deal with this guy. And there were other people making similar claims, so I think he was getting frustrated with the whole process. I had prepped him, I don't know, three or four hours, and I had prepped him on prior occasions for similar depositions, so there was nothing new at all. But he has a self-proclaimed reputation for being arrogant, which is definitely truth in advertising. We sit down at the deposition, and—I guess to give you a little more background, this is a guy who, [during a break in] a prior deposition, had turned on his laptop, and done a quick internet search of some site that lists the wealthiest Americans under forty, and he was checking to see where he was that day. I looked over and I said, "What are you doing?" [*Laughing.*]

But in this deposition, it started out, and the opposing counsel was a pretty relaxed guy, somebody who used to be a securities litigator at [a big firm] and was now solo and handling smaller cases. A decent guy and not that aggressive, but big. He started to ask questions, and they were *basic* questions, like where do you live and that kind of thing. And my client was being utterly resistant and recalcitrant in every way. He would not give him his home address, he wouldn't give him his wife's name, kids, and the guy was really just kind of doing a generic opening session. At some point [*laughing*], the opposing counsel said to him, "Is there a problem with what's going on or is there some reason why you can't answer my questions? They're not that complicated." That kind of thing.

And my client says, "Yeah, there is a problem. You stink. Your fucking face stinks." When you're defending a deposition you're pretty attentive—I couldn't jump on him fast enough. I was just in shock. [*Laughing.*] I went off the record right away and took him outside and read him the riot act. I think lots of people defending depositions coach their witnesses pretty aggressively, and I try to avoid doing that, certainly in depositions. I want to prep them well, but I don't want to be telling them what to say or pushing them hard in the dep, because it always comes through I think. But I took him outside and just railed at him, because it was stunning, I didn't know what—I mean the court reporter [*laughing*], I looked at the court reporter and said, "That isn't in your thesaurus, is it?" He was just in shock. He was a court reporter I'd used before, and he was looking at me like, "Oh, my God, what is this guy doing?"

So we came back in, and the opposing counsel was actually very cool about it. He sort of laughed, and he saw it as being advantageous to him, and it didn't really bother him. He wasn't personally insulted. I think, in retrospect, I was so surprised, what I should've had the guy do was to come back in and immediately go into this prostrate position and apologize for his brain tumor acting up or something. But we went back in, and we had started up the dep again, and I said something to the opposing counsel about let's turn this to something relevant, and he couldn't resist—his first question back on the record is, "So what is it about my face that stinks?" Just picking the scab. [*Laughing.*] But we moved him on pretty quickly, and

from that point on [during every break in the deposition for the rest of the day] we discussed settlement. At the end of the day, we in fact settled. Literally, every break, we'd talk about it and
negotiate, and at the end of the day we settled, and
did so very advantageously to the client.

[*Laughing.*] But it was a thing where, there was
no way I wanted to let that day go without getting
it settled. I didn't want to see that deposition [tran-
script] ever.

{Interviewer:} Because you knew you would.

I knew I was going to see it in every pleading
that ever went in front of the court. It didn't matter
if he was asking for an extension of time to file
something, he'd submit that as an exhibit. [*Laughing.*] It made my guy look worse than he'd ever
been depicted [by] any of the plaintiffs in these
related cases. And confirmed the worst fears. . . .
The thing is, the upside was, I just had no problem
telling him that he was going to settle, and he was
going to settle at this offer which was reasonable. It
was like, we're not going to debate this. It has to be
done now.

*{Interviewer:} Maybe you should encourage your clients to
do that more often. {Laughing.}*

Well, you know, it really does give you lever-
age to tell them what you think is appropriate.
'Cause he did feel badly, just a little bit, for sort of
having irritated me. That was I think the only
thing he felt. He was sorry he'd perturbed me.
[*Laughing.*] I did keep the rough transcript on my
bulletin board for some time. [*Laughing.*]

CHAPTER FOUR

Planting the Flag

The litigator is obligated to attest that the legal positions taken by the client have a reasonable basis in fact or are based upon reasonable belief. The litigator is not obligated, however, to believe in the client or the legal positions taken by the client. No rule or other authority or pressure could accomplish that end. The litigator may do an extraordinarily effective job representing a client without believing in the client or the client's legal position. Still, in practice, litigators want to believe in the legal position taken by the client and in the client itself—and, by and large, they do.

Some individual litigators, as a matter of personal policy, choose not to represent this or that client.

> There are some clients I would not do work for. Period. And we have some clients at the law firm that [other] people don't want to do work for. I do work for one client that I believe . . . many people in the law firm would not want to do work for because of what their political views and positions are.

Some firms choose not to represent this or that client because the representation would be morally troublesome for individuals within the firm or because the client would present a public relations problem. Thus, an individual litigator or a firm may choose not to represent, say, manufacturers of cigarettes, operators of pornography websites, or logging companies, even if the representation would be lucrative or the legal work would be interesting. These decisions are rare, however, and take place at the margins of litigation practice. Also, such choices are easier to make when the decision maker does not face financial pressures to accept as a client anyone who can pay.

Litigators who either do not have the luxury of choosing clients or who are willing to suspend judgment in undertaking the representation nevertheless look for some moral justification for the representation. One litigator says, "I have to be able to find some moral ground to plant my flag in for me to be comfortable with the representation." Another says, "I don't have to necessarily believe in the client himself, because [for example] I'm working on a case right now where I've never met the client, but I do have to believe in the client's position. Somehow." Some litigators refer to finding something to believe in as "rationalization." The litigator using this term means to be, at least to a degree, self-derogatory. He uses it when, even though he can articulate a basis for providing the representation, some discomfort remains. Sometimes the moral dissonance experienced by the litigator is severe.

Litigators find that their job is more satisfying when they believe in the client or the client's position. They also find that having a reason to believe makes them more intellectually curious and motivated. These comments by one recently retired litigator and one in midcareer are typical:

- I never really felt it was a necessity that I "believe" in the client's substantive position. On the other hand, this is a sliding scale. The less heinous the client's putative actions, the easier the representation always was. And in fact, I often found myself believing that the client's position was the proper one.

- Perhaps not surprisingly, in most cases I believe my client is mostly in the right, which probably indicates that I am subject to being convinced by my own arguments. And the more strongly I believe in the "rightness" of my client's position, the more personal commitment I am likely to bring to the case. To what extent that personal commitment affects the quality of my representation is hard to say.

Litigation is a propitious field of endeavor for those who have a vital need for moral justification of their work. The litigator can always "find some moral ground to plant [his] flag in."

I don't think I have ever, and maybe *ever* is a strong word, but nothing has come to mind where I ever thought a case that I was involved in was that unambiguous. The importance of that, I think, is, for me at least, there's always something—there has always been something that I can believe in about a client's case. . . . There's very little that I've seen that I'd call black and white. . . . As I say, I haven't been able to find a situation where there wasn't something that I could fight for. There may be parts of a case that I believe in more than other

parts, but there's always something in the case that
I've been able to latch onto and feel good and self-
righteous about. [*Laughing.*]

Finding something to believe in may require looking
beyond surface impressions, but that is exactly what litigators are trained to do and what litigation is designed
to force.

> I try to really understand the client's perspective,
> and even if at first blush it seems to be a position
> that I'm going to have a hard time believing in,
> what I find is if you look hard enough and you open
> your mind enough, you typically can find, again,
> some moral ground that you can believe in.

Every case is unique and presents its own unique
grounds for moral justification of the representation,
though some means of justification are common. The
most common means of finding something to believe in
with respect to representation of a client are considerations of overall fairness, examination of particular legal
issues, cold assessments of money values, and scrutiny of
the other side.

Making an overall assessment of the equities of the
dispute is not a legal analysis, though the litigator trans-
lates it into one. Sometimes the litigator realizes that a
potential outcome, even one that would be consistent
with his own personal preferences, would not necessarily
be fair.

> For instance, right now I'm working on a brand-
> name drug against generics, and quite frankly, all I
> do is purchase generic drugs. But I'm representing

the brand-name drug, and I can *rationalize* it . . . by
saying, well, they spent millions of dollars in
research and development and now it's payback
time. So, again I've somehow rationalized a position
which, if I really thought about it, my first instinct
was one of distaste, I've now somehow played a
mind game [through which] I actually can justify
everything I do and also feel good when I do it
well.

The commitment of a legal wrong not only causes harm
but also creates opportunity. In some cases, the litigator
defending a wrongdoer realizes that the aims of the
opportunists, if realized, would not necessarily be fair.

For example, in the environmental context, sometimes you have to represent the bad guy, the guy
who caused the pollution. And what I've learned is
that, particularly in the environmental context, in
many instances, the regulators are taking such a
strict position, such a stringent interpretation of a
rule, that, in fact, yes, the client did do *x,* but,
number one, it's clear that it wasn't intentional,
number two, it's clear that they did everything they
could to prevent it, and number three, it's clear
that nobody got hurt, blah blah blah blah blah. So,
is it really appropriate to hit them with penalties
that are going to cripple the company?
And I'll give you a really good example of
where that one—I worked on a matter involving a
refinery, and the refinery was fairly close to a residential area—there was a school nearby, there was a
residential area nearby. And one day while a worker
was just doing regular maintenance on some pipes

at the facility, they opened a valve on a line that they thought was empty, and it wasn't empty, and it squirted some stuff out that was not terribly toxic, but had just an amazingly strong odor. And it was a strong enough odor that the odor carried across the property line and, you know, some people that lived nearby claimed that they got nauseous from the odor. And, you know, that's the kind of thing that sometimes regulators will get all excited about, even if it's just crystal clear that nobody was made sick or injured or anything, and, you know, I guess all of this is a very long-winded way of saying it's a rare day that you can't find some moral ground that's worth defending for a client.

The litigator can also find something to believe in through resort to legal analysis. This method comes easily because part of the litigator's job is to break down the case into its separate legal issues and because the legal issues in every case are multitudinous and technical.

The litigation process itself is a process of rationalization. It conforms messy, ambiguous problems and disputes to standardized procedures and rules of law. To speak with someone involved in a conflict both before and after he is exposed to lawyers and the litigation process is revealing: beforehand he speaks impressionistically and in vernacular, whereas afterward he tends to adopt the vocabulary and framework of the law. For instance, a property owner whose land is taken by the government for a government project first speaks of getting paid a fair price, but later speaks of "just compensation" and "highest and best use." The litigator plays an integral role in rationalizing the dispute, relating it to legal categories. The pushing and shoving of litigation is to a large extent a fight over how to categorize the dispute under the law—a determination upon which the outcome depends. The litigator who employs legal analysis to rationalize representation of a client tracks the rationalizing processes of the litigation itself.

Generally, every case poses several legal issues from among many categories, including, to name only a few, jurisdiction (Does this court have the authority to decide this case?), discovery (What information is each party entitled to obtain from the other parties, and how?), liability (What standards of conduct have been legally determined to apply to this situation, and, under the facts, have those standards been satisfied?), construction of statutes (What does this statutory provision mean?), and admissibility of expert testimony (Is this witness qualified to testify as an expert, and on what issues is this expert entitled to give an opinion?). Novel types of legal issues are virtually nonexistent. Because the circumstances of every case are different, however, the combinations of issues vary from case to case, and the specific legal issues in each case are different. For example, the issue of liability for breach of contract is generally familiar to the litigator and the courts, but each contract dispute involves different parties, different contract terms, different intent, a different situation under which the contract is entered, and so on. Consequently, the specific legal issue in each contract dispute—whether there is liability for breach of contract in *this* case—is different.

Furthermore, lawsuits typically involve multiple legal claims or "causes of action"—the grounds on which, under the law, some sort of relief such as damages may be granted. For example, a party fundamentally asserting a breach of contract claim may include a claim for fraud. A case that fundamentally concerns ownership of intellectual property rights may include claims not only for trademark and copyright violations but also breach of contract, breach of fiduciary duty, negligence, and fraud. A case that fundamentally concerns a real estate investment gone bad may include claims for negligence, fraud, and violations of consumer-protection and even securities laws. Finally, each legal issue, whether a procedural issue like jurisdiction or a substantive claim like breach of contract, is likely to consist of several subissues. Thus, the question whether there is liability for breach of contract raises the questions whether the parties are competent to enter a contract, whether there was an offer, whether there was acceptance, whether there was consideration, whether the contract is permissible under law, whether there was a breach, whether there are damages, whether there are defenses, and so on. Each of these subissues is a separate legal issue. Thus, every case presents a multitude of discrete, unique legal issues.

Legal issues are technical in that their analysis involves the application and manipulation of rules and of language. The creation, interpretation, and application of legal rules is a matter of drawing lines. The meaning of words is contextual—a matter of drawing lines, too. To the litigator, President Clinton's famous response to a question before a grand jury, "It depends on what the meaning of the word 'is' is,"[1] makes perfect sense and, indeed, has a certain beauty. The meaning of rules—how to interpret and to apply them—and the meaning of words are up for grabs in every case.

Thus, in every case, the number and variety of legal issues and the technical nature of legal analysis give the litigator ample opportunity to form judgments and to make arguments about where the lines should be drawn. The litigator can always fashion an argument that the line should not be drawn where the other party proposes to draw it—that is the litigator's stock in trade. In any given case, this or that single legal issue or even all the legal issues together may not induce any moral fervor in the litigator. The parties to the lawsuit may disagree, but the litigator may consider the legal positions taken by each party to be within reason. Such circumstances present no moral qualms to the litigator. Even if the legal positions taken by each of the parties are reasonable, though, the litigator may develop a strong sense of the rightness of the client's position because the litigator tends to believe in his own arguments, usually worked out through consultation with the client, and because even in a simple case so much is at stake. Where the line is drawn will have real-life consequences: money will flow or not, power will settle or shift, jobs and careers will continue or not, the reputations of individuals and organizations will rise or fall, policies will persist or change, companies will survive or crumble. The outcome of a private lawsuit affects parties outside it, too. The outcome affects the law itself, and in the future the law will be used in ways both anticipated and unforeseen.

In some cases, also, the litigator may have a strong personal sense of right and wrong with respect to the proper legal analysis of a particular issue. The litigator may have a heightened sense of the proper outcome of a particular legal issue because he analyzes legal issues all the time: he has a sense of legal context. Though the litigator's personal sense of where a line should be drawn under the law is immaterial to the resolution of the legal issue, it nevertheless may provide moral support in opposing, on behalf of the client, the other party's argument as to where the line should be drawn.

In some instances, either the opposing party's position on a legal issue or the status of the law itself appears unreasonable, which certainly gives the litigator something to believe in on behalf of the client. It may be the central issue in the case:

> The firm already represents [Jones], [Jones] needs local counsel, has been using local counsel here in [this state] that they're not entirely satisfied with, and they've been talking to our office about handling some of their defense work, tobacco litigation defense. And it's something that none of us have ever done before and that [this office] hasn't been involved in before. . . . When I heard about it, I was troubled by it. And I was particularly troubled because if we were defending a tobacco company and trying to help a tobacco company win the argument that smoking doesn't cause cancer—I was going to be really uncomfortable with that. Or denying that they had covered it up, or any of the stuff that happened back in the sixties or seventies. . . .
>
> And so we as a department had a meeting and discussed whether we were willing to be tobacco industry lawyers. And we actually did an unusually in-depth due diligence investigation of the types of cases that they would be referring to us, and that type of thing. And basically what became clear to us was that this particular tobacco company, [Jones], was not one of the companies that was still denying that smoking caused cancer or that it was

bad for you—in fact, that's not the state of that litigation today, at least not as it involves this client. And that, in fact, this client was defending against individual smoker lawsuits where the issue in the case was simply: Did the smoking cause this person to get sick or was it another cause, and what should the smoker really get if they started smoking *after* the surgeon general's warnings were on the cigarette packs?

In other words, it's one thing if you started smoking in the days when the cigarette companies were still saying it doesn't have any adverse health effects and it doesn't make anybody sick. But if you started smoking in the seventies or eighties, when it was sort of like, Duh!, you know, how much is any individual smoker really entitled to if they make a voluntary choice to smoke in the face of the surgeon general's warnings? . . . And in some cases, [plaintiffs are] people for whom the cancer could easily have been related to their jobs. Like, in one instance, [the plaintiff was] an oil refinery worker, and [he was] constantly around hazardous petroleum vapors and benzene and things like that, and there really was a very legitimate question of whether the smoking was responsible for [his] cancer. [Jones's] point simply was: "Look, we don't deny that smoking can cause cancer, but this guy worked in an oil refinery for thirty years, why are we liable as opposed to his employer? Shouldn't there be some level of causation required in a case like this?" . . .

And although I haven't been asked to work on these cases yet, when I actually heard the cigarette company's side of the issue, I was able to find what

I considered to be some moral ground worth
defending, and in my mind, the moral ground
worth defending was that people need to take some
responsibility for their own actions. . . . You know,
there were some really, really interesting legal
questions about—it was very clear that there were
some liberal judges in [this state] that were essentially vitiating the causation requirement in these
tobacco cases. And I think that's wrong. Just, without even getting to the moral issues, as a lawyer I
believe it's important to establish good law in [this
state], and I simply felt that there were some
judges that were making some really bad law in the
interest of reaching what they felt was the right
moral result. So that's how I deal with the issue.

In some instances, the other party's legal position may
appear reasonable on some legal issues but not on others.
Just as filing a lawsuit does not mean the lawsuit has
merit, asserting a particular claim or taking a position on
a particular issue does not mean that the claim or the
position taken is valid. Sometimes the litigator may consider one or more claims asserted by a party to be not
only disputable but also absurd.

One case I did . . . was a licensing case, where the
company we represented—this guy was supposed
to develop this software for [the company]. And he
never really quite developed it the way it was supposed to be developed. So our client stopped paying
him the money. It was a term of months that we
were supposed to be paying, for a number of years.
So the guy who developed the stuff sued the client.

He sued not only for the money he didn't get paid, but he asserted a fraud claim, that the client had intentionally done this deal to take his product off the market, so that he would basically not be able to sell it to somebody else, and they could develop their own internal product and wouldn't have a competitor—some ridiculous theory like that.

So, we were having a hard time settling the case, and we did an arbitration. The other side brought in their main witness—the guy had died, and the widow owned the claim. So she came in, and we brought in some of the employees who had worked on this product. We went for the day, and it was interesting, because at the end of the day, they probably were entitled to the money under the contract, but the fraud claim was ridiculous. The arbitrator gave us a quick gut feedback on how it went. He said, "The contract claim is tough, I'll have to think about that one," and he explained what the issues were and what he was thinking about.

So when he finished I asked him, I said, "What about the fraud claim?" And he looked at me and he put his fingers in a zero and he goes, "Zero on the fraud claim." And he looked at the woman . . . and he just held up his hands for her. He said, "Zero. That fraud claim is going nowhere. Do you think any jury in the world is going to look at these four witnesses and think they tried to commit a fraud? Forget it. That fraud claim is gone." And that's kind of how I feel about a lot of this stuff. Most people who are just going in to do their work aren't out there trying to cook up frauds. They're

just not. They're trying to do their jobs, mistakes
happen, and people attach these fraud claims all the
time, with no real basis for it.

Focusing on a limited set of legal issues may enable
the litigator to abide more troubling aspects of the case.

The firm had [a client, an environmental cleanup
company, Acme]. What they did was they took . . .
waste materials from other [businesses] and basically were a disposal site. The problem was that the
[government agency] felt that they were illegally
disposing of these wastes, that they were basically
taking these wastes and, rather than doing proper
disposal, they were just stockpiling them in tanks
and piles. They had a pile of oily dirt and they had
tanks, huge tanks full of [waste], and the government thought it was just one big sham illegal disposal operation, where they were taking money and
then not doing anything with the waste.
   Well, to the extent that they were guilty of
that, it's obviously something I'm going to be
pretty uncomfortable about, because, number one,
just on moral grounds I would have a real problem
with that, but beyond that, my practice has always
tended to push cleanups. I tend to sue oil companies and make them clean up contaminated
groundwater plumes that they've created and
things like that. . . .
   So, what I found in this instance was that they
had overfiled or overcharged—the [government
agency] had brought this 240-count civil complaint against [Acme], and it was wildly redun-
dant, they were accusing them of things that were

clearly not illegal, and they were trying to cram the activity under some code provision that clearly did-n't apply, and so the position I took was that, OK, [Acme], it looks like you were doing some things wrong—and, by the way, I later found out that a couple of things they were doing really were just blatantly illegal, and we didn't know they were doing it. They actually, two of their employees ended up getting charged criminally, and I think they even went to jail. But it was pretty clear that some of the employees were taking money on the side to do some of this stuff. And there was no cor-porate ratification of the illegal conduct.

Anyway, this was clearly the kind of case that I was uncomfortable with and that created some sort of moral problem for me, and I was never comfort-able working on the case. The way I was able to get comfortable with it was, I convinced the client to focus its efforts on attacking the clearly erroneous portion of the complaint. What typically happens in these cases is that the defendant agrees to pay a penalty and/or change parts of its business opera-tion without admitting guilt or wrongdoing. Thus, for purposes of settlement, you "admit without admitting" the allegations for which you appear most likely to be found guilty, and your litigation/settlement strategy is to pare down those claims as much as possible, so that you redefine the ballpark of settlement negotiations. With the client's approval, I found the claims in the com-plaint that clearly were wrong and attacked those, and said, look, if you're going to nail these guys—basically my attitude was, look, [government agency], if you're going to nail these guys, at least nail them for what they really did wrong, don't throw in two hundred other counts for things that they really didn't do wrong. And so that's how I kind of dealt with that situation.

In some instances, a single legal issue may in the litigator's mind cast a shadow over the rest of the case, providing the litigator with moral shade.

For instance . . . there's this huge case with Japanese slave labor camps. Basically there's a Japanese firm and during World War II they had used a lot of the Chinese prisoners as basically slave labor. And the suit was brought in the United States. . . . Naturally [*laughing*] our firm represents the Japanese slave labor firm, and all these associates got stuck on it. Horrible work. I was friends with quite a few of them, and I thought that was just horrible, especially being Asian, there was no way I was going to stick my finger in that case—and I was just lucky I was busy with [a different horrible case]! [*Laughing.*]
    Anyway, my friends were working on it, and a lot of them just felt horrible—who wants to be obviously on the wrong side of a human rights issue? It was just particularly unsavory. And I noticed the way they all rationalized it, and the way they all rationalized it was one way, which was the easiest way. In order for them to *believe* the fact that they're representing this Japanese firm that had done horrible things, they were saying: "This is the United States. Is the United States the correct jurisdiction to be dealing with issues . . . which are entirely dealing with events forty years ago, in

Japan, dealing with *Chinese* prisoners?"—you know—"This case was brought by *Chinese* descendants who—descendants of these prisoners—because many of them are not even alive anymore—it's like their *granddaughter* bringing it, who's now living in America, and who's trying to get it through some subsidiary of this Japanese firm." So it's like, you know, "We're completely off the turf."

So they devoted themselves to the specific legal issue of jurisdiction. And I saw that *they* were doing it, and I started realizing that I think that, especially with junior associates, who maybe are a little more idealistic than the lawyers a little bit down the line who have probably worked on so many terrible cases that they've stopped it—it's that they do this. They find kind of a *rationalization,* a *reason,* to *believe* in their client because I think fundamentally we *want* to believe in our client, and I think we feel the need for it—I do. I certainly do, but then I play these dumb games with myself.

The issue of money almost always gives the litigator a reason to believe in the representation. Most cases are about money, if only because money is how the civil law usually gives a wronged party relief. The distribution of money can arouse a sense of right and wrong as surely as any other issue, and litigation often puts large amounts of money on the table.

I might think the client sure could have handled this contract better, but do they deserve to be paying a hundred million dollars damages because of the stuff that went wrong? You know, *no.* I don't believe that they should.

Even where a wrong admittedly has been committed and the only issue in the case is money, the matter can still be complex. The party that has been wronged may seek not only money but also vindication, solace, revenge, or a host of other possible satisfactions. The litigator defending a wrongdoer knows that the fact that a wrong has been committed does not mean that whatever the injured party demands in return is right.

Sometimes you have cases where you sit down, you get the complaint filed, you do your factual investigation, and you look at the law, and you sit down in a room and the lawyers look at each other and say, "Hey, OK. We have a liability here. So we're fighting over damages now, right?" And then you sit down and you realize that the fight *is* about damages. It's pretty clear there is going to be a liability. Now, they may have appended a bunch of claims that are nonsense claims, but they've got a good claim, and the question becomes, "OK, do they get the four hundred million they think they should get, or do they only get the twenty-five million we think they should get?" And that's what you're litigating about for the next couple of years, as you develop the facts and work on your damage analyses and have your experts and things like that. . . .

It's really kind of risk management. I don't think I've ever yet had a case where a client got sued and a lot of money is demanded, and the client walks in and says, "Well, we got sued for this amount of money, we think we should just pay it." That just doesn't happen. [*Laughing.*] It's never that simple. There's always other stuff added on top of it. Sometimes in a collection action you can see stuff like that, people come in and say, "Hey, you owe me fifty thousand bucks." But, even some of those, they'll throw fraud claims on top of them. I'm doing one now like that. There's no *fraud.* The guy didn't have the money, they didn't pay the bill! [*Laughing.*] So, a case that was pretty simple has a fraud claim in it.

A demand for money that seems absurd minimizes qualms that under other circumstances might be significant.

I should say, this guy, even though he wasn't always above board, I always, actually in every single situation, felt that he was actually—you know, maybe there was some claim a plaintiff would have against him, but it was never anywhere close to what the plaintiffs were actually trying to get. Like somebody had a claim worth a thousand dollars, fifteen hundred dollars, something like that—realistically—and they were making claims of, you know, thirty million. So, even as I saw him as being kind of a problem, . . . it never became a significant moral issue.

Sometimes the litigator finds moral solace by looking at the other side. The identity and conduct of the other side may appease the litigator's concerns about his own client. This method is the last resort but is almost always fruitful.

There certainly have been instances where I have had very mixed feelings about the client. Where I have not necessarily *despised* the client [*laughing*], although maybe if I think hard enough I could find some cases of that, but there certainly have been cases where there have been things about the client that I really have not liked. I guess my, thinking back on it, my way of rationalizing those thoughts is that, in at least most of those cases, the other side has been even worse. [*Laughing.*]

So maybe my client is not someone who I believe in, in an absolute sense, but they certainly are a whole lot better than the other side. That's, in my view, not the way to live your life, but it has been something I've used to get through the day, if you understand what I'm saying. . . . When I said the other side was even worse, sometimes it's the other client and sometimes it's the other counsel and sometimes it's both. I remember several years ago where . . . one of my colleagues was heavily involved in doing work for a guy who basically admitted that he was unscrupulous and untrust-worthy. And he [*laughing*], he proved that! The other side, both the opposing party and the other lawyer— . . . *they* were so bad that it made my guy look *decent.*

Among litigators, distaste for opposing counsel is common. In major cities, even the litigation subsection of the bar is now so large that litigators know only a handful of their counterparts around town to any meaningful degree. The era of the close bar is past, as are its advantages—the development of customs and common courtesies, observance of the Golden Rule, the sense of professional community. Litigation practice tends to be impersonal and often bitter. Many litigators appear to

believe that they have a duty to obfuscate issues, oppose
legitimate discovery requests, make inaccurate representations to the court, and take every opportunity to make
life and work difficult for opposing counsel. Some degree
of enmity may exist even when opposing counsel acts
professionally, because the interests of counsel for different parties conflict and because conflict tends to become
personalized. Instances in which opposing counsel
appear to take advantage of the process solely for personal enrichment, and which thus provide support for
the most cynical estimations of the profession, especially
arouse the litigator's moral indignation.

> I have worked for two and a half years, against my
> will, I spent probably 60 percent of my time on a
> securities case. And I had no intention of working
> on securities. One of the reasons I stayed on it was I
> was working for a woman partner who I really
> enjoyed working for. I basically had never worked
> with a woman in a power position like that before.
> We had a very good relationship. So even though I
> didn't like the work, she gave me a lot of responsi-
> bility, really good work.
>   The problem with the case—the case itself was
> very unsavory in my opinion. It was a securities
> case—we naturally were defendants—so it was your
> typical securities investment fraud kind of action
> where limited partners in a limited partnership
> were alleging that basically the partnership was
> ripping them off, not giving them the returns they
> were supposed to get [*laughing*] and also deliber-
> ately running the company into the ground, right?
> So they could just milk as much money as possi-
> ble—it was a very typical securities class action.

We represented defendants and, quite frankly, I thought [the] defendants—they were scum. . . .

God, first they had targeted these—practically all the investors were these *eighty*-year-old—unbelievable—eighty-year-olds in retirement homes in Florida, OK? They'd gone out and gotten all these people to dump like a thousand dollars of *retirement* money in this bogus limited partnership, and they had thousands of investors around the country, and they didn't give them the returns. You can say anything to an eighty-year-old guy, and from what I can gather their marketing was just disgusting. It sounded like a pack of lies. They said, "Oh, you know, we can guarantee you a 10 percent return and more," and they could barely squeeze out 3. Unbelievable. And so it was a very typical securities fraud case. And even meeting the president, who was like a multimillionaire—I mean it was just so obvious. I just felt they were a big bunch of, like, scum. So, these are all our clients, and I had no faith in them. [*Laughing.*]

And, the *plaintiffs* though, it was interesting. Even though individual plaintiffs were—I felt terrible for them [but] the case had been brought by—there's a lot of these plaintiffs' firms in Florida. Apparently there's several in Florida, because I consistently saw—because I was Miss Legal Research Queen—I consistently saw the same firms. There's five firms around the country which are *very* well known. Plaintiffs' security, kind of class action, derivative action kind of suits, and they're famous for them, and that's how they made their money. They bring many of them and all they need to do is—they're basically pushing for settlement. . . .

They aren't bringing it because they're really [*sarcastically*] *seeking justice.* They're trying to get settlement, because then they get a huge cut out of it. Frequently what happens, this recently happened to me and my credit card. I guess there's all these class actions against credit cards for, like, fees. For every class action that happens it's something like every dollar in settlement, there was some figure that was quoted, literally the actual plaintiffs, the actual people, receive something like two cents for every dollar or something, and everything else goes to the lawyers. I can't remember the figures, but something horrible like that.

So this case was brought by this firm that was one of those top five firms [*laughing*] which brings hundreds of these suits. So, when I first got on the case, I got this sinking feeling like, "Oh, this is terrible, gosh, this is the worst thing I [could] work on, I'm representing this completely *scummy* firm." Like I wanted all of the CEOs and all the people on the board to go to jail forever. They were that bad. But then I realized that the case had been brought by an *equally*—this is all a mind game—an *equally* skanky firm that specialized in bringing a lot of these suits, many of which were sham suits. I don't think this case, this suit was actually a sham suit [*laughing*], but I was sitting there thinking, "Well, this plaintiffs' firm has brought many sham suits." And actually a lot of the cases [brought] by these firms were getting tossed out [by the courts] because they were just basically a big bunch of bullshit. And then I started thinking, well, you know, they sit there and they talk about the retirees who've been defrauded, but, quite frankly, the retirees have lost their thousand-dollar investment and they might be able to get like two bucks back after the end of the settlement.

So then I sat in on the settlements and I saw the way how the lawyers were dealing with settlements, and it was really—like, our side, the lawyers were very jaded. They're like, we know what these lawyers want, they want a cut out of the pie. They just want to also be sure they can cover their butts by . . . making sure the judge will approve the settlement and won't take that as obviously just for personal gain, right? There has to be something in it for the actual plaintiffs. So . . . I think that I do what a lot of, I've noticed, young attorneys do, like a lot of my other friends who are junior associates, I think we do a lot of rationalization. Yes, it's important to us that we believe in our client, but even if our client is terrible, I think we play a lot of mind games in order to ensure that we don't feel bad about representing them. Does that make sense?

Another type that the litigator sometimes encounters on the other side is the True Believer. This type may be the opposing party or opposing counsel, or both. The True Believer believes absolutely that his cause is morally right and that he occupies and has an exclusive claim upon the moral high ground. He lacks subtlety of vision, seeing everything associated with opposition or indifference to his cause as monolithically evil. He believes his own propaganda. The True Believer is a self-righteous opportunist. He parlays a wrong, real or perceived, into a moral basis for advancing his interests, which he then pursues with a Machiavellian disregard for moral particulars. The True Believer uses his belief in his

moral superiority to justify or excuse his own unscrupulous conduct in the litigation. The presence of the True
Believer on the other side gives the litigator ample
grounds to feel good about representing his own client.

The litigator, with respect to each case on which he
works, needs only a small patch of ground in which to
plant his flag, only the narrowest opportunity to find
some moral basis for proceeding with the representation.
Each case, however, usually presents the litigator with
ample space and opportunity for moral justification.
Almost every case presents some combination of potential unfairness, debatable legal issues, ridiculous
demands for money, and questionable conduct by the
other side.

CHAPTER FIVE

Enforced Realism

The litigator's appearance and reputation as a Hired Gun are deceptive. The litigator's interests are not coextensive with the client's, and the litigator's sense of right and wrong may have little or nothing to do with the client's. Even when the litigator's moral view is consistent with the client's, it derives from a different source than the client or the paycheck. It derives from the work. The object of the litigator's work and the medium of his practice are the cases, and the cases—the facts, the civil procedure, the substantive law, and their interplay—are complex.

Litigation does not fabricate complexity. Litigation does not constitute a hermetically sealed world, with its own exclusive logic, experience, and moral realm. Cases are complex because the reality of social affairs is complex.

First, the litigation process reveals the obscurity, contradictoriness, and ambiguity of social reality. The ambiguity may occur at the level of facts—the who-what-when-where kinds of determinations that serve as the basis for legal consequences. It occurs also at the levels of meaning and implication: ambiguity occurs even without intentional deception by witnesses and despite the black-and-white of words printed on a page.

One of the things I've learned is that two reasonable, intelligent people can see the same set of events in a very different manner. And it is possible for two different people to tell a very different story about what's happened, without either of them really lying. I think that people are—certainly you do run into just outright liars sometimes, and that's unfortunate. I have been amazed at how differently two individuals can absorb the same events. And when they describe what they've witnessed, it comes out differently.

The difficulty of establishing facts concerning even seemingly simple occurrences increases dramatically as the interests of the participants and observers increase.

I mean, this is not anything profound, but you and I stand at the intersection and watch a car wreck, and your description could be completely different than mine, even if we're both impartial observers. So, you become used to the fact that there is surprisingly little that is completely, clearly, and unambiguously true. Or that you can establish as that. I guess, again, it's partly because it's a human process. Different people perceive things in different ways, colored by their self-interest and their experiences, and so forth and so on, and so it can be surprisingly difficult to determine what the truth is and to get evidence and people agreeing on what the truth is.

Memory and meaning shift as circumstances shift.

From having taken hundreds of depositions and reviewed endless boxes of documents, I realize that

memory is very fallible and plastic. Most of us have
the conceit that what we remember is accurate.
Often it isn't, especially when there are strong
incentives—generally money—or emotions tugging the recollection one way or another. . . .
Money exerts an astonishing tug on what people
think and what they are willing to do.

The elasticity of memory and narrative recollection, the
invariable ambiguities of words and documents, the
kaleidoscopic nature of reality, the mutation of circumstances, and the variability of meaning are the stuff of litigation.

One thing I am convinced of, and being a litigator
has convinced me of this, is that people really do
hear things the way they want to hear 'em and see
things the way they want to see 'em. You can have
five people in a room listening to the same argument, and those five people are going to describe
it differently, and they're going to attribute different motives, different blame, and different
credit to the same argument. And in my mind
that's what litigation is really all about. It's
almost always fighting over the gray area or the
nuance or, you know, one person assumed one
thing, another person assumed another thing, and
that's why it hit the fan. Or, after the agreement
was reached, the circumstances changed in a
significant way, such that one party felt that the
only fair way to deal with it was x, and the other
party felt that the only fair way to deal with it
was y. In those cases, yeah, truth comes out, but
I really feel like almost every case I get involved
in you're dealing with the gray area.

The intense and pitiless examination of witnesses and documents, the obsessive scrutiny of circumstances that are part of the litigator's job exploit the uncertainties at the heart of social life itself.

Second, the law and the litigation process reveal the disorderliness of social reality. Society is not uniform. Its actors do not act uniformly. Social life is neither rational nor still. As convoluted and confounding as the litigation process may seem, it is radically oversimplified and rationalized compared to the chaotic and competing interests and concerns that it is designed to serve. Every regulation, every standard, every rule, and every procedural device exists to serve some societal interest. Often the rule or the procedure misses its mark, sometimes by a treacherous margin, but the law and the litigation process are also always in flux. Every regulation, standard, rule, and procedure is constantly under attack and subject to modification. That challenge comes with every case. The law struggles to keep pace with the unceasingly inventive demands and ever-changing relationships of society.

The work of litigation trains the litigator to see the complexity—to see people, organizations, institutions, action, motivation, and phenomena for what they are rather than what they claim to be. It teaches that appearances may be and usually are deceiving, if only because appearances usually do not adequately represent either the essence or the whole.

> There was litigation [in the form of] a whole variety of class actions against every major wood products producer in the country for the various kinds of composite woods they put together. And, no question, some of those woods, certain batches, certain times, certain products, did not perform as they were sup-

posed to. But a number of these class actions got resolved so that there was an individual claims process, and you would have these endless individual hearings on damages, and a lot of those were equally absurd. People had put out money to get a composite wood product and suddenly were making claims as if they wanted teak everywhere. And I guess that is the kind of bigger thing about the work, is just the sense of kind of enforced realism.

{Interviewer:} Meaning?

Meaning I don't think there's very much that's Romantic, with a capital R, about law. I think it's much more of a daily lesson in realism.

{Interviewer:} Again, what do you mean by "realism"? Other than not Romantic.

I mean a kind of unvarnished sense of what people do, what people want, what companies do, what companies want, you know? There is no—the way in which, for example, branding in advertising creates images of companies in our head. Those have no bearing and no reality at all when you do work for those companies.

The work becomes not only the source but also the object of the litigator's realist consciousness. Litigation practice makes the litigator a skeptic.

This consciousness extends to matters of right and wrong and of good and evil. The True Believer who is litigation counsel has learned nothing from litigation. Litigation practice teaches that right and wrong is not a function of form or identity. Money, power, status, ethnicity, color, gender, plaintiff, defendant, and other crude means of identification are not per se indices of moral quality. The work teaches that right and wrong is a matter of precision: it must be understood contextually, and its dimensions must be carefully measured. The litigator's moral consciousness incorporates the countervailing and divergent elements, acknowledging their rightful place in the scene.

For example, a corporation is not evil because it is a corporation. Its status as a corporation does not guarantee that any conduct undertaken in its name is wrong. The fact that a corporation appears to have done wrong or that another party alleges that it has done wrong does not mean that it did. The fact that it has done wrong under the law in one respect does not mean it has done wrong in other respects. The fact that a corporation has committed a wrong does not mean the wronged party is therefore right in all respects. The fact that a corporation has done wrong also does not mean that it forfeits all claims to justice.

Litigation practice teaches that those who claim or appear to have moral superiority sometimes have an imperfect basis for it or no basis at all. Sometimes those who claim right are nothing more than schemers or bullies. Sometimes wronged parties use their claims to mask their own complicity. Sometimes they were indeed wronged, but their conduct in the resulting, changed circumstances is hardly irreproachable. Sometimes those who have been wronged abuse their moral advantage.

Litigation practice teaches that those who appear virtuous or blameless may be selfish, vindictive, or harmful. It teaches that those who claim some large, selfless social awareness, who purport to advance the interests of society, may be self-interested. It teaches that moral righteousness is a luxury if not a fraud.

The mark of full consciousness of the lessons of litigation practice is the understanding that doing good may cause harm. Vindicating a wrong, for example, may cause damage. Imposing a policy to advance one interest may impede or destroy others. It may destroy the wrongdoer. Changing the wrongdoer to correct harm may so affect its capacity and essence as to make it altogether different, severing its historical and contemporary ties and scuttling its institutional knowledge. It may create new opportunities for some but close or foreclose them for others. Bystanders may suffer in the fallout.

Through the lens of litigation practice, common moral pieties appear inelegant, and expressions of moral outrage lose their luster. The work promotes the recognition and acceptance of complexity: that even when one side is right, other sides may be right also; that to be right is not necessarily to be absolutely right; that prevailing in a conflict does not necessarily mean that one is right. Litigation practice cultivates the exercise of restraint in moral judgment, the ability to hold conflicting moral judgments simultaneously, the understanding that the experience of moral dissonance may be appropriate in that it accurately reflects real conditions, and the awareness that resolution of moral conflict may be self-deceiving.

> So much of the mischief in life and in the law is the result of people who are too sure they are right. Being a litigator has taught me something about seeing both sides of an issue, even if I am paid to argue only one. So I think a spirit of humility and skepticism is as close as I would come to a creed.

The awareness of uncertainty and complexity, more than any other condition or force, provides the litigator with the moral authority for doing his work, for proceeding with the representation of a client in a lawsuit.

One does not have to engage in litigation practice to acquire a sense of realism or to develop a consciousness of moral complexity. In any organization or social environment, at least some people develop the awareness that the public representations and images of the organization or the particular social environment are deceptive. The distinction of litigation practice, though—in contrast to other occupations—is that the work very nearly forces the practitioner to see through images and representations. Working on the cases—and all that such work entails—forges a consciousness of moral complexity.

Still, not every litigator has the consciousness of a realist or employs it at all times. Some litigators see people, organizations, events, and phenomena only for what they claim to be or for what they are not. Some see right and wrong only in terms of ethical requirements, their own self-interest or, indeed, the client's interests. Some may understand complexity and yet be given to the belief that he is absolutely right or to fits of moral outrage.

The enforced realism of litigation practice is complete: it leaves no illusions about the workings of the law, either. Piousness typically accompanies invocation of the legal process, and the law self-reverently clothes itself in the high-minded rhetoric of justice and truth. The litigator knows better. His work experience constantly exposes the law to be a matter more prosaic.

Your sense of, say, the . . . majesty of the court takes a big tumble when you go in front of [a certain federal judge]. I got an order a couple of days ago where a [different] federal judge in [state *A*] denied a motion we had brought on jurisdiction. And it's just a piece of shit. I mean, he could deny our motion in lots of different ways. But, instead, he puts out a forty-page opinion drafted by some clerk who can't write coherently and, more importantly, notwithstanding the length, [there is] *nothing but* sloppy reasoning. You know, if *a* equals *b,* then *b* equals *x* kind of logic. And literally that bald on the page. You don't even have to try to infer that it's there. And you say to yourself, *"This person is a federal judge?"* And I think it's either the person's not bright or he's lazy. And I think it's the latter. And how do you tell your client? You're in federal court, [so supposedly] you're going to get a good judge, you're going to get a smart judge, you're going to get a hearing—it's one thing to try to guess legal risk, but it's another thing when you have to look at the opinion and tell your client, "Well, actually the judge didn't understand, or didn't pay attention, or didn't read it."

Every litigator likely experiences the bad decision or, worse, the bad judge. This encounter is not the situation in which a judge makes a decision adverse to the client, not a matter of a judge rejecting the litigator's argument in favor of another. It is not a matter of the judge being meddlesome or aloof, liberal or conservative. It is, rather, the situation that betrays the judge's ignorance of the facts or the law, or both. It is the situation that suggests the judge is motivated by something—who knows what?—outside the bounds understood by the parties and the attorneys, that indicates that the judge has not considered carefully the dispute at hand. Even litigators whose clients benefit from a bad judge or a bad decision recognize it as such.

The trouble is that the success and legitimacy of the legal process depend on judges. An error in judgment by a judge is acceptable, but a dereliction of duty is not. Society requires that judges as a body perform very well on balance, and in individual cases the parties' need for a good judge ranges from crucial to desperate. The legal process assumes that the judge will be impartial and wise, or at least not lazy or corrupt, yet judges have the virtues and flaws of human nature. Sometimes they make mistakes. Sometimes their inspiration remains obscure. Now and then, they are not conscientious.

> I have become since practicing more acutely aware that law is—there's an academic term for this, I might not have this right, but I was going to say the realpolitik, or maybe it's realism. Realism. I think I'm using this right. . . . What I mean by that is that the process is not a computer that takes inputs, computes things, and spits out output. The human factor is enormous. In my view, and this can be overstated because it just depends, for instance, on what judge you have and stuff, but I would not have guessed how important the human factor, as distinguished from the actual law, I would not have guessed how important the human factor is. By that I mean, you know, there are jurisdictions or judges where you simply don't want to be a defen-dant. I'm sure it's the same from the plaintiff's side. Where you'll have a judge who will be told the law and will then go on a mission to get around the law because that judge wants a certain outcome, rather

than just sitting down and trying to impartially view the law. You know, how often do juries make decisions for reasons that are divorced from the sheer logic of law or the compulsion of the facts? It happens frequently. Not all the time. I'm not suggesting this is the case all the time, but . . . when I started out, I think I was very surprised to find that there were some judges that just really weren't that interested in your brief. And all the compelling logic you put together. They were reacting to something else.

{Interviewer:} What has been your sense of what they were reacting to?

It just varies. It could be that somebody's the out-of-town lawyer, coming in and trying to tell this judge what to do. It could be that the judge has previously dealt with one of the lawyers and doesn't like him. You know, they were at each other's throats. It could be *anything.* It could be that he saw a movie last night and a character he didn't like in the movie was wearing the same suit you're wearing. There's no end to what it could be. But I just think that there are frequently situations where you're getting a judge responding to something other than just the sheer law and the sheer facts. I think it's just that's the way human beings are. Some human beings are going to be better at focusing on legal argument, facts, and what the research shows the decision should be. Some are going to be better able to set aside prejudices that they possess. There is going to be this human factor in the system that a lawyer can't control. That's, I guess, the significant point in all of this.

The processes of selecting and appointing judges seek to restrict the position to those who will perform well. Succeeding in the judicial selection process does not, however, make one competent as a judge. Certain procedural rules, the appeals process, the parties in a given case, the estimation of colleagues and practicing attorneys, the prospect of advancement, and pride all serve to pressure judges to make good decisions, but the effectiveness of such checks and balances has limits.

The legal process depends on proper functioning of all its elements—not just judges, but juries, witnesses, lawyers, and parties. The litigator sees the ordinariness in the functioning of all these elements. The out-of-control witness, for example, is a common phenomenon. The litigator can spend hours and days over a period of months and years talking to a witness, seeking to understand the witness's information and to prepare the witness for a deposition or trial, only to see the witness turn into an alien in the courtroom.

> If you're going in to a trial, what you want more than anything is to be able to tell your story in a coherent, straightforward style and have complete control over your story. Well, you *can't.* Your witness, your star witness could get there and just completely lose it. [*Laughing.*] That's happened to all of us. You just think, this person's in great shape. They're prepared, they've thought about it, they've got a good demeanor, and then they get up there, and you're sitting there thinking, "Who *is* this guy?" [In] the first jury trial that I had by myself, I had one witness who was essential to the case, who I was so worried about, had some things that he had to explain, and I just didn't know how

well he'd explain them. On the other hand, I had
his boss, who was a thoughtful, intelligent guy, not
old, but older than the other one I was talking
about, and didn't have that much baggage to carry
in terms of what he was going to testify to. We get
to trial, and the guy I'm worried about is great, he
completely connects with the jury, explains himself
well, is likeable, is nice, and is Mr. Sure Thing. The
other guy is pausing between his answers, and I
could tell he's just trying to think, but it makes
him look like he's evasive, and it came out completely the opposite of what I thought it was going
to be. And that's the human element of it.

A common wisdom of litigation practice is that
juries are unpredictable. One never knows in advance in
whose favor a jury will decide a case or why it will reach
the result it does. The danger of this wisdom lies not in
the truth that one can never know in advance what
another will do, much less what a group will do, but in
its implication that a jury may not act rationally. If any
two juries may decide the same case differently, if the
evidence in a case appears to favor one party but a jury
finds in favor of another, if juries are capricious, then the
process is a hoax. The unpredictability of juries is anti-
thetical to the promise of the legal process, but the
process recognizes this and seeks to minimize the potential damage. The selection and performance of juries, like
that of judges, is subject to some rationalization and control. For example, the judge and the lawyers for the parties have the opportunity to screen for and dismiss
potential jurors who appear incapable of deciding a case
based on the evidence presented and the instructions
given. Rulings by the judge may limit the jury's expo-

sure to evidence, and instructions from the judge guide the jury's analysis of the evidence. These are crude instruments, however, and, even if a jury does its job properly, solely focusing on proper evidence and following instructions, the outcome is not predictable. A small industry of outside consultants has grown to exploit the unpredictability of juries. Academics build entire careers attempting to rationalize the decisions of juries. Lawyers, more than anyone, exploit the irrationality of juries and the latitude of jury decisions. They attempt to influence the jury's decision in countless ways outside the bounds of formal evidence and argument, from the cut and color of their suit on the first day of jury selection to the deliberately improper remark in closing argument.

The litigator or client who does not heed the common wisdom sets himself up for a hard lesson. Even litigators who understand juries must sometimes endure grim reminders.

> And then you get jurors. A juror might just, for whatever reason, really like one of the lawyers, and then they're going to be more inclined to fight for that lawyer's side. . . . I just had a jury trial recently that ended up a hung jury, and it went 10–2 our way. And it went 10–2 within half an hour. And they stayed out for seven days, I think. And the reports we got back were that the two that went against us just flat refused to talk to anybody else. The others were trying to engage them and explained why they had their point of view, tried to get them to argue, but they just flat out refused to deliberate. There was some speculation, I don't know if it's true, on the part of some of the jurors

that—the two holdouts were women, and there was some speculation that those two women were offended by some of the men and would never bring themselves to vote for those men. Now, does that have anything to do with the logic of the law? Absolutely not. It's just nothing. It's something that's completely beyond the control of lawyers. So, that's just another example. So much of it is beyond your control. So much more than I would have ever guessed coming out of law school. It can be enormously frustrating. You spend all this time and something silly is going on that you could not have anticipated and you couldn't have done anything about.

Sometimes the legal process works approximately as it is supposed to work. At other times, though, as the litigator knows more than anyone, it is just nothing. When the legal process malfunctions, the consequences for one or another party may be calamitous.

To the litigator, however, the truth about the legal process—that it does not always work as it claims and that its actual workings remain obscure—is no different from the truth about other institutions, organizations, and individuals. The truth fills the litigator with neither joy nor dread.

Whatever one calls the realism, it differs from cynicism, which can be bred by the same sort of work exposure, but which I think results from lazy thinking and an unwillingness to get into the gray zone. To have no particular illusions about the workings of lawyers, corporations, and the system of litigation is not synonymous with an absence of hope or bitterness. Rather, as an example, it's understanding the judicial system as it deals with commercial disputes to be fundamentally a dispute resolution process that permits civil society and is thus eminently worthwhile—as opposed to some higher search for abstract values of "truth" and "justice."

To the litigator, the truth about the legal process is the starting point for participation in it, for fighting on behalf of a client.

AUTHOR'S NOTE

I was told the Two Rules of Practice in the late morning of my first day of practicing law. Sitting at my desk in my assigned quarters, in the offices of a large firm, in a downtown skyscraper in a major West Coast city, I was briefly describing my first work assignment to the partner who had recruited me to the firm and who had come to greet me. The partner, a litigator, was modest and good-natured in demeanor. Through direct experience and observation, I eventually discovered this partner to be, as I had suspected upon first meeting him, an outstanding lawyer. The full dimensions of my first assignment were as yet unclear to me. The partner listened courteously, imparted the Two Rules with a wry smile and without elaboration, and then pulled me away for lunch.

To my recollection, the two of us never again discussed the Two Rules until years later, when I set about to write this essay, but from that first day forward, through various work experiences, I reflected on that moment. Hearing the Two Rules in such a setting from such a source fired my curiosity about how the litigator sees the world and therefore about the nature of the litigator's moral consciousness.

My work experience is typical of the litigator. Over approximately ten years, I have worked in two different cities, in two large firms and two small ones. Like all litigators with at least minimal experience, I have represented all manner of clients, in all manner of cases regarding all manner of legal issues, in all phases of litigation in various state and federal courts. I have worked with and against litigators of a range of styles and temperaments. I have read and heard countless opinions, decisions, orders, and judgments from trial and appeals courts, arbitrators, and quasi-judicial officers. I have directly observed countless episodes in the work experiences of colleagues and all manner of incidental scenes that one comes across in the course of practice. During that time, I have engaged in hundreds of conversations of varying length, formality, and intensity, in a variety of places and situations, with clients, colleagues, passing acquaintances, and adversaries, regarding the lessons of litigation.

Upon deciding to undertake this study, I asked a few litigators to reflect on their experiences and careers and to discuss them with me in an interview format. Eventually I conducted interviews with eight litigators. Each of the interviewees has extensive experience working in firms with a reputation for providing high-quality legal services and has led a successful career in litigation practice. I had directly worked with one of the interviewees on cases; at one time or another, three others had been colleagues in the same workplace, though we never worked directly together; and I have never worked or been professionally associated with the remaining four. Collectively, the interviewees have worked as litigators in major cities across the United States over the past four decades, covering the full range of years of litigation experience: from a fourth-year associate, through junior partners, to senior partners and one retired former partner. The primary reason, however, that I asked these particular lawyers to discuss with me the lessons of litigation is that I knew each one to be an excellent litigator.

The interviews were conducted between June and November 2001. Initially, six interviews were conducted verbally (tape-recorded and later transcribed), one was conducted in written form, and one both verbally and in writing. Several of the initial interviews were supplemented by follow-up conversations, verbally and in writing. The tape-recorded interviews lasted approximately one to two-and-a-half hours each.

I first transcribed the tape-recorded interviews verbatim. The punctuation reflects my effort to be faithful to the syntax and rhythm of the interviewee's speech. All emphases indicated by nonbracketed italics are the speaker's.

In incorporating material from the transcripts and written interview responses, my obvious preference has been to quote the interviewees in full on a given subject, to allow the interviewees to speak for themselves. Occasionally, certain considerations necessitated my editorial interference. All ellipses indicate my own deletion of extraneous verbiage for purposes of brevity and clarity. All brackets indicate my interference, either to simplify a tangled passage; to clarify a reference; to conceal the identity of the interviewees, other lawyers, clients, law firms, and judges; or to note supplemental information such as laughter or a particular kind of emphasis.

Each of the interviewees reviewed drafts of the manuscript and provided comments and criticism. I also circulated drafts to several others—litigators, nonlitigator lawyers, and nonlawyers—for comments.

Notes

Introduction

1. In 1921, Learned Hand commented: "I must say that as a litigant I should dread a lawsuit beyond almost anything else short of sickness and death." Learned Hand, The Deficiencies of Trials to Reach the Heart of the Matter, Address before the Association of the Bar of the City of New York (Nov. 17, 1921), *in* 3 LECTURES ON LEGAL TOPICS 87, 105 (1926). Hand's appreciation of the dreadfulness of lawsuits contributed to his greatness as a judge.

2. Every lawyer is bound by the official ethical rules of the profession in each state in which he practices. The ethical rules vary in particulars from state to state. Practicing lawyers also commonly refer to the American Bar Association's Model Rules of Professional Conduct. The broad limits on the lawyer's primary duty to the client generally relate to the lawyer's obligations as an officer of the court and as a public citizen.

1. The Lawyer in American Society

1. This understanding of Tocqueville's sense of the virtues of the old order and the challenge of democracy is based on Phillips Bradley, *A Historical Essay, in* 2 ALEXIS DE TOCQUEVILLE, DEMOCRACY IN AMERICA 370 (Phillips Bradley ed., Vintage Books 1990) (1840); DORIS S. GOLDSTEIN, TRIAL OF FAITH: RELIGION AND POLITICS IN TOCQUEVILLE'S THOUGHT (1975); ANDRÉ JARDIN, TOCQUEVILLE: A BIOGRAPHY (Lydia Davis with Robert Hemenway trans., 1988) (1984); Harvey C. Mansfield & Delba Winthrop, *Editor's Introduction* to ALEXIS DE TOCQUEVILLE, DEMOCRACY IN AMER-

ICA, at xvii (Harvey C. Mansfield & Delba Winthrop eds. & trans., Univ. of Chicago Press 2000) (1835, 1840); and especially on Tocqueville's own introduction to his study, ALEXIS DE TOCQUEVILLE, DEMOCRACY IN AMERICA 3–15 (Harvey C. Mansfield & Delba Winthrop eds. & trans., Univ. of Chicago Press 2000) (1835, 1840). Tocqueville's preoccupation with public morality as a component of his complex thought is discussed particularly in Goldstein, *supra* at 87–88, 128. Tocqueville's concern with greatness is discussed particularly in Mansfield & Winthrop, *supra* at xxiii–xxix.

2. Jardin, *supra* note 1, at 3–36.

3. *Id.* at 35–36, 54.

4. Tocqueville wrote about the episode in a letter to a confidante in 1857, reproduced in part in Jardin, *supra* note 1, at 61. In the letter, Tocqueville does not identify the works he read, but his biographer reports that the Tocqueville library, which has survived, includes few modern works other than those of Voltaire, Montesquieu, Buffon, Rousseau, Mably, and Raynal. *Id.* at 62. Also, in 1836, Tocqueville wrote privately that Montesquieu and Rousseau, along with the seventeenth-century philosopher Pascal, were daily influences on his thought. Mansfield & Winthrop, *supra* note 1, at xxx.

5. Tocqueville and Beaumont's report was first published in France as DU SYSTÈME PÉNITENTIAIRE AUX ÉTATS-UNIS ET SON APPLICATION EN FRANCE (Paris, H. Fournier 1833) and in the United States as THE PENITENTIARY SYSTEM IN THE UNITED STATES AND ITS APPLICATION IN FRANCE (Philadelphia, Carey, Lea and Blanchard 1833). See Bradley, *supra* note 1, at 374 n.2.

6. The classic account of Tocqueville and Beaumont's travels through the United States is GEORGE WILSON PIERSON, TOCQUEVILLE IN AMERICA (Johns Hopkins Univ. Press 1996) (1938).

7. *See generally* ROBERT V. REMINI, ANDREW JACKSON AND THE COURSE OF AMERICAN EMPIRE, 1767–1821 (1977).

8. ROBERT V. REMINI, ANDREW JACKSON AND THE COURSE OF AMERICAN FREEDOM, 1822–1832, at 83–99 (1981).

9. *Id.* at 172–78.

10. For the details of Jackson's presidency, see *id.* at 181–392; ROBERT V. REMINI, ANDREW JACKSON AND THE COURSE OF AMERICAN DEMOCRACY, 1833–1845, at 1–419 (1984).

11. Tocqueville, *supra* note 1, at 12–15.

12. Alexis de Tocqueville to M. Stoffels (Feb. 21, 1835), *in* 1 MEMOIRS, LETTERS, AND REMAINS OF ALEXIS DE TOCQUEVILLE 397 (M. C. M. Simpson ed., London, Macmillan 1861), *quoted in* Bradley, *supra* note 1, at 383–84.

13. Tocqueville, *supra* note 1, at 251–52.

14. *Id.* at 252.

15. *Id.*

16. *Id.* at 256.

17. *Id.*

18. ROSCOE POUND, THE LAWYER FROM ANTIQUITY TO MODERN TIMES 221–49 (1953).

19. DAVID HAWARD BAIN, EMPIRE EXPRESS: BUILDING THE FIRST TRANSCONTINENTAL RAILROAD 663 (1999).

20. JAMES WILLARD HURST, THE GROWTH OF AMERICAN LAW: THE LAW MAKERS 302 (1950).

21. Pound, *supra* note 18, at 254.

22. EDMUND IONS, JAMES BRYCE AND AMERICAN DEMOCRACY, 1870–1922, at 19–141 (1968).

23. 2 JAMES BRYCE, THE AMERICAN COMMONWEALTH 481–94 (London, Macmillan 1889).

24. Bryce somewhat contradicted himself on this point in writing elsewhere that lawyers had a generally favorable influence on public opinion—they helped to educate the public on legal aspects of public issues and consequences of legislation. 2 Bryce, *supra* note 23, at 263–64.

25. Louis D. Brandeis, The Opportunity in Law, Address to the Harvard Ethical Society (May 4, 1905), *in* BUSINESS— A PROFESSION 329–43 (1914).

26. Woodrow Wilson, The Lawyer and the Community, Address to the American Bar Association (Aug. 31, 1910), *in* 21 THE PAPERS OF WOODROW WILSON 64 (Arthur S. Link ed., 1976).

27. Brandeis, *supra* note 25, at 337.

28. This concern informs a variety of critiques of lawyers over the balance of the twentieth century. *See, e.g.,* THERON G. STRONG, LANDMARKS OF A LAWYER'S LIFETIME 353, 377–78 (1914); A. A. Berle Jr., *Modern Legal Profession, in* 9 ENCYCLOPAEDIA OF THE SOCIAL SCIENCES 340 (1933); Karl N. Llewellyn, *The Crafts of Law Re-Valued,* 28 AM. BAR ASS'N J. 801 (1942); MARK J. GREEN, THE OTHER GOVERNMENT: THE UNSEEN POWER OF WASHINGTON LAWYERS (Norton rev. ed. 1978) (1975).

29. Deborah J. Cantrell, *A Short History of Poverty Lawyers in the United States,* 5 LOYOLA J. PUB. INTEREST L. 13 (2003) follows the development of this portion of the bar to the present day.

30. K. N. Llewellyn, *The Bar Specializes—With What Results?,* 167 ANNALS AM. ACAD. POL. & SOC. SCI. 177 (1933), despite its title, concerns not so much specialization as the thorough fragmentation of the bar by the early 1930s.

31. JEROLD S. AUERBACH, UNEQUAL JUSTICE: LAWYERS AND SOCIAL CHANGE IN MODERN AMERICA 158–230 (1976), contains valuable information regarding the origins and dynamics of the legal practice in and around the federal government during the New Deal.

32. Charles A. Horsky explored this world from the perspective of the private lawyer in a series of lectures published as THE WASHINGTON LAWYER (1952).

33. JERRY L. MASHAW & DAVID L. HARFST, THE STRUGGLE FOR AUTO SAFETY 5 (1990) (citing M. BERNSTEIN, REGULATION BY INDEPENDENT COMMISSION (1955); G. KOLKO, THE TRIUMPH OF CONSERVATISM (1963)).

34. *See* Mark J. Green, *The Perils of Public Interest Law,* THE NEW REPUBLIC, Sept. 20, 1975, at 20, 22. *See generally* Edward Berlin et al., *Public Interest Law,* 38 GEO. WASH. L. REV. 675 (1970); Charles L. Halpern & John M. Cunningham, *Reflections on the New Public Interest Law: Theory and Practice at the Center for Law and Social Policy,* 59 GEORGETOWN L.J. 1095 (1970); *The New Public Interest Lawyers,* 79 YALE L.J. 1069 (1970); F. RAYMOND MARKS, THE LAWYER, THE PUBLIC,

AND PROFESSIONAL RESPONSIBILITY (1972); Robert L. Rabin, *Lawyers for Social Change: Perspectives on Public Interest Law,* 28 STANFORD L. REV. 207 (1976).

35. Austin Sarat & Stuart Scheingold, *Cause Lawyering and the Reproduction of Professional Authority: An Introduction, in* CAUSE LAWYERING: POLITICAL COMMITMENTS AND PROFESSIONAL RESPONSIBILITIES 3, 3–4 (Austin Sarat & Stuart Scheingold eds., 1998).

36. Robert T. Swaine, *Impact of Big Business on the Profession: An Answer to Critics of the Modern Bar,* 35 AM. BAR ASS'N J. 89 (1949); 2 ROBERT T. SWAINE, THE CRAVATH FIRM AND ITS PREDECESSORS, 1819–1948, at 466 (1948).

37. K. N. LLEWELLYN, THE BRAMBLE BUSH: ON OUR LAW AND ITS STUDY 19–76 (Oceana 1996) (1951).

38. *Id.* at 75.

39. Hurst, *supra* note 20, at 335–59.

40. *See* Horsky, *supra* note 32.

41. *See* Geoffrey C. Hazard Jr., *The American Lawyer Today and Tomorrow* (unpublished) (on file with author).

2. The Judicial Process

1. *See* 1 WILLIAM BLACKSTONE, COMMENTARIES *3–*37.

2. *Id.* at *69.

3. *Id.* at *69, *71.

4. *Id.* at *69.

5. *Id.* at *69–*70.

6. *Id.* at *70.

7. *Id.* at *71.

8. C. C. Langdell, *Preface* to A SELECTION OF CASES ON THE LAW OF CONTRACTS v, vi (Boston, Little, Brown 1871).

9. *Id.* at vi–vii.

10. For an anecdotal account of the dramatic impact of Cardozo's 1921 lectures, see Arthur L. Corbin, *The Judicial Process Revisited: Introduction,* 71 YALE L.J. 195, 196–98 (1961). Corbin's report of Cardozo's response to the immediate demand that the lecture series be published indicates Cardozo's awareness of their revolutionary effect: "He said that he

did not 'dare to have it published.' Half seriously, he added: 'If it were published, I would be impeached.'" *Id.* at 198.

11. BENJAMIN N. CARDOZO, THE NATURE OF THE JUDICIAL PROCESS 10–11 (1921) (hereinafter JUDICIAL PROCESS).

12. *Id.* at 12–13.

13. *Id.* at 18.

14. *Id.* at 31.

15. *Id.* at 71–72.

16. *Id.* at 98.

17. *Id.* at 129.

18. *Id.* at 115.

19. *Id.* at 133–34.

20. *Id.* at 143.

21. *Id.* at 150.

22. *Id.* at 22–23, 161.

23. BENJAMIN N. CARDOZO, THE GROWTH OF THE LAW 69–70 (1924) (footnote omitted).

24. CARDOZO, JUDICIAL PROCESS, *supra* note 11, at 173, 179.

25. *Id.* at 113.

26. For an extensive list of judges' commentaries on judging, from the time of Cardozo's lectures through most of the balance of the twentieth century, see Shirley S. Abrahamson et al., *Judges on Judging: A Bibliography,* 24 ST. MARY'S L.J. 995 (1993). For a partial list of outsiders' attempts to illuminate judicial decision making, see Shirley S. Abrahamson, *Judging in the Quiet of the Storm,* 24 ST. MARY'S L.J. 965, 966 n.5 (1993).

27. CARDOZO, JUDICIAL PROCESS, *supra* note 11, at 22.

28. Felix Frankfurter, Some Reflections on the Reading of Statutes, Address before the Association of the Bar of the City of New York (March 18, 1947), *in* 47 COLUM. L. REV. 527 (1947).

29. Marbury v. Madison, 1 Cranch 137 (U.S. 1803).

30. Frankfurter, *supra* note 28, at 529.

31. *Id.* at 544.

32. Learned Hand, Is There a Common Will, Address

before the American Law Institute (May 11, 1929), *in* 28 MICH. L. REV. 46 (1929).

4. Planting the Flag

1. *Testing of a President: Excerpts from Clinton's Grand Jury Testimony as Quoted in Starr's Report to Congress,* N.Y. TIMES, Sept. 17, 1998, at A28.

Index